CorelD

Training Guide

CorelDRAW 12
Training Guide

By
Satish Jain
Wing Commander (Retd.)
B.Sc. B.E. (Electronics), M.E.(I.I.Sc.) M.Tech. (I.I.T. Kanpur)

Shashank Jain
B.E. (Delhi College of Engineering)

BPB PUBLICATIONS
B-14, CONNAUGHT PLACE, NEW DELHI-110001

FIRST EDITION 2006

Distributors:

MICRO BOOK CENTRE
2, City Centre, CG Road,
Near Swastic Char Rasta,
AHMEDABAD-380009 Phone: 26421611

COMPUTER BOOK CENTRE
12, Shrungar Shopping Centre, M.G. Road,
BANGALORE-560001 Phone: 5587923, 5584641

MICRO BOOKS
Shanti Niketan Building, 8, Camac Street,
KOLKATTA-700017 Phone: 22826518, 22826519

BUSINESS PROMOTION BUREAU
8/1, Ritchie Street, Mount Road,
CHENNAI-600002 Phone: 28410796, 28550491

DECCAN AGENCIES
4-3-329, Bank Street,
HYDERABAD-500195
Phone: 24756400, 24756967

MICRO MEDIA
Shop No. 5, Mahendra Chambers, 150 D.N. Road,
Next to Capital Cinema V.T. (C.S.T.) Station,
MUMBAI-400001 Ph.: 22078296, 22078297

BPB PUBLICATIONS
B-14, Connaught Place, **NEW DELHI-110001**
Phone: 23325760, 23723393, 23737742

INFO TECH
G-2, Sidhartha Building, 96 Nehru Place,
NEW DELHI-110019
Phone: 26438245, 26415092, 26234208

INFO TECH
Shop No. 2, F-38, South Extension Part-1
NEW DELHI-110049
Phone: 24691288, 24641941

BPB BOOK CENTRE
376, Old Lajpat Rai Market,
DELHI-110006 PHONE: 23861747

LIMITS OF LIABILITY AND DISCLAIMER OF WARRANTY

The Author and Publisher of this book have tried their best to ensure that the programmes, procedures and functions contained in the book are correct. However, the author and the publishers make no warranty of any kind, expressed or implied, with regard to these programmes or the documentation contained in the book. The author and publishers shall not be liable in any event of any damages, incidental or consequential, in connection with, or arising out of the furnishing, performance or use of these programmes, procedures and functions. Product name mentioned are use for identifications purposes only and may be trademarks of their respective companies.

All trademarks referred to in the book are acknowledged as properties of their respective owners.

Price : Rs. 75/-

ISBN 81-8333-101-7

Published by Manish Jain for BPB Publications, B-14, Connaught Place,
New Delhi-110 001 and Printed by him at Akash Press, Delhi.

PERFACE

The objective of this Training Guide is to meet the growing need of the users in exploring this CoreDRAW 12, highly versatile Graphic package in easy-to-understand language. It is observed that most of the books available in the market do not explain CorelDRAW 12 in step-by-step training manner from the first time user's point of view.

CorelDRAW 12 is a package that enables you to design vector graphics as well as bitmapped graphics at equal ease. Most of the capabilities of this package are explained in this training guide with illustration. A very useful feature of this book is that different types of tools in CorelDRAW 12 are explained with practical examples, so as to enable a reader to understand them without any outside help.

This training guide is comprehensive in covering different features of CorelDRAW 12. It is hoped that all the needs of a first time user of CorelDRAW would be met by this book. This book can also serve as a useful reference book for experienced users.

The design, production and testing of examples of this book were completely carried out by Ms. Geetha Iyer and Mrs. Anita of Printek India, New Delhi and we thankfully acknowledge their contribution.

We shall feel obliged to the readers if they send us their critical opinion of the presentation, readability and coverage in this book and send us suggestions in improving the subject matter.

1st November, 2005   Authors

About the Authors

Mr. Shashank Jain obtained his Bachelor of Engineering degree from Delhi College of Engineering New Delhi. Mr. Jain is a freelance software trainer with wide experience in organizing training program at various levels. He has authored six books on PC software and Windows operating sytems. Presently, he is working on Windows XP and Office XP packages and Windows 2003 Advance Server Network systems.

Wing Commander Satish Jain (Retd) obtained his B.Sc. degree from Agra University in First Division and is a gold medal winner. He also received National Scholarship awarded by Government of India. He obtained his B.E. (Electronics) degree from the Indian Institute of Science, Bangalore (I.I.Sc) with distinction. He joined Indian Air Force as Technical Officer and held different appointments during 21 years of service career. He was specially selected by the IAF to undergo Master of Engineering course in Aerospace Sciences at the I.I.Sc, Bangalore and Computer Engineering at the Indian Institute of Technology, Kanpur.

By virtue of his wide experience in the field of computer science and engineering, he was positioned by the IAF as the Deputy Director in the Planning Cell of Technical Training of the Air Force Officers and Airmen at Air Headquarters, New Delhi. He has organized many courses and seminars in computer science for national bodies like Institution of Electronics & Telecommunication Engineers (India), The Institute of Cost and Works Accountants of India (ICWA), National Productivity Council and Directorate General of Resettlement, Ministry of Defence, Government of India. He is Professor(IT) in IIT&M at Janakpuri New Delhi and has authored over twenty five books on various subjects pertaining to computer science.

CONTENTS

"Live as if you are going to die tomorrow. Learn as if you are going to live forever."

"Progress is impossible without change; and those who cannot change their mind cannot change anything."

— George Bernard Shaw

CHAPTER 1

CorelDRAW 12 Basics

Introduction

CorelDRAW 12 is a very powerful graphic design package. With that, comes a fairly useful design environment and many combination of tools and effects. In this book you will learn to work with most of these tools and effects.

Computer graphics programs are classified in two categories. The first type are bitmapped programs like Adobe Photoshop, etc. wherein the images are created in the form of bitmap. The other set of graphic programs use vector graphics where the graphics are composed of mathematical curves. CorelDRAW belong to the category of vector graphic program. In addition, CorelDRAW 12 comes packaged with Corel PHOTO-PAINT, a powerful program for creating and editing bitmap images also.

Before you start creating your own graphic images, you need to understand a few basic concepts about what CorelDRAW 12 does—both on your screen and behind the scenes.

A basic understanding of the unique way in which CorelDRAW creates images will help you to design images and transform those images to print copy or Web page output more effectively.

CorelDRAW 12 is a vector-based program, which means that it creates and handles images as mathematically defined vectors. Vectors are objects with both *magnitude* (size) and *direction* (angles, curvature, and so on). The files that store CorelDRAW 12 images consist of lists of lines, with information on their location, direction, length, colour, and curves.

Note: Defining images as a series of vectors is a more efficient way to work with them than defining images as bitmap or a huge number of individual pixels. This is because even a simple object might have thousands of pixels, each individually defined, whereas the same image might be defined more rationally as a small number of curve segments.

CorelDRAW 12 vector image files are often smaller than comparable bitmapped image files. A bit map file of 2724 KB will be just of 112 KB in CorelDRAW because it is using vectors.

In addition to creating more compact files, CorelDRAW 12's vector-based images have other important advantages. You can easily resize a CorelDRAW image to a thumbnail sketch or icon or a billboard-sized graphic. When you change the size of a bitmap image, you lose *quality* because the number of dots, or pixels, remains the same even as the illustration is enlarged. That is not the case with CorelDRAW's curve-based illustration. It will not get distorted.

However, graphic designers have to work with bitmaps, especially while working with images that appear in, or as Web pages. Popular Web browsers cannot interpret images created in CorelDRAW's native format. The relatively low resolution of computer monitors (generally 72 dots per inch) tends to negate the advantages of creating vector-based images. The relatively small, low-resolution images seen on Web sites tend to make curves jagged and grainy regardless of how smooth and high-resolution the original image is.

CorelDRAW gives you the capability of creating almost any graphic image file you will ever need. Most of the images are still destined for hard copy, and CorelDRAW's vector-based images are best for printed output. Corel's vector based tools provide the most powerful range of features for designing images. CorelDRAW can then easily translate those images into bitmap formats. In fact, CorelDRAW has a powerful capacity to transform objects into both of the Web-compatible bitmap file format: i.e. GIF and JPEG.

CorelDRAW Terminology

Before you get started in CorelDRAW 12, you should be familiar with the following terms.

Object An independent element that you can modify. Objects include images, shapes, lines, curves, symbols, text and layers.

Drawing The work you create in CorelDRAW; for example, custom artwork, calendars, posters and newsletters.

Docker window A window containing available commands in a dialog box that remains open as you work.

Flyouts A button which when clicked opens a group of related tools.

Scrapbook A folder filled with clipart, photos, fills, outlines, FTP sites and other items you can use in your drawings.

Thumbnails Small, low resolution representations of images.

Artistic text A type of text to which you can apply special effects, such as shadows.

Paragraph text A type of text that you can use to add blocks of text, which is useful for drawings such as brochures.

Starting CorelDRAW 12

To start CorelDRAW, do this:

1. Click the Start menu, highlight Programs, highlight CorelDRAW 12 and then click on CorelDRAW 12 as shown in Figure 1.1.

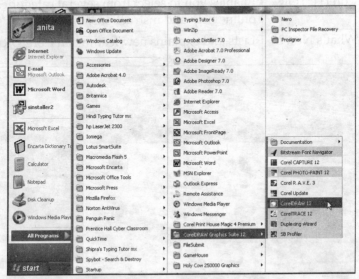

Figure 1.1   Starting CorelDRAW 12

2. The Welcome window appears as shown in Figure 1.2.

CorelDRAW Interface

The Getting Started window (See Figure 1.2) provides six options for getting started with CorelDRAW 12, as explained in Table 1.1.

Table 1.1   Starting Options

Icon	Name	What it Does
	New	Creates a new window in which you can design a graphic.
	Recently Used	Opens recently used graphic image files you worked on.
	Open	Opens the Open Drawing dialog box, enabling you to select from any saved graphic image file.

(Contd...)

Icon	Name	What it Does
🖨	New From Template	Enables you to choose from a list of pre-designed page templates that you can use as a basis to begin a design.
🍎	CorelTUTOR	Enables you to select from several categories of online help and instructions.
⊕?	What's New?	Lists and explains new features in CorelDRAW 12

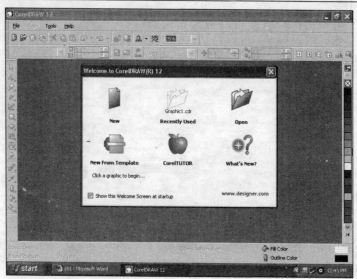

Figure 1.2 Starting with the Welcome Window

To create a new graphic image from scratch, click the New Graphic icon in the Welcome Window to CorelDRAW dialog box. When you do, you will see an empty CorelDRAW 12 window, such as in Figure 1.3.

Title Bar

The Title bar appears at the top of the CorelDRAW Window. The Title bar shows the name of the file you are currently working on. When the size of the window is less than the maximum size, you can move the entire window by clicking on the title bar and dragging the mouse to a new position.

Menu Bar

The Menu bar is located below the Title Bar and contains the Pull Down

Menus. The Pull-down menus contain the CorelDRAW commands. Click on a menu title in the menu bar to pull down the menu.

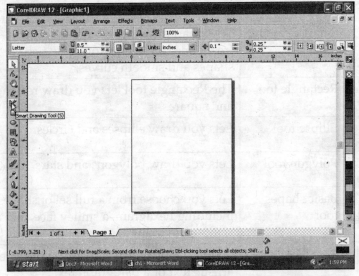

Figure 1.3 An Empty CorelDRAW window

Tool Box

The toolbox is located to the left of the Drawing window and contains the tools to create and edit graphic objects. When you move the cursor over any of the tools in the toolbox, a ToolTip will appear identifying that tool. (See Figure 1.3)

The various tools available in the tool box are explained below in Table 1.2.

Table 1.2 Tolls in Tool box and their description

Tool	Name	Description
	Pick tool	Lets you select and transform objects.
	Shape tool	The Shape tool lets you edit the shape of objects.
	Zoom tool	The Zoom tool lets you change the magnification level in the Drawing window.

(Contd...)

Tool	Name	Description
	Freehand tool	The Freehand tool lets you draw lines and curves using mouse.
	Smart Drawing tool	The Smart drawing tool converts the freehand strokes that you draw to basic shapes and smooth curves.
	Rectangle tool	The Rectangle tool lets you draw rectangles and squares.
	Ellipse tool	Lets you draw ellipses and circles.
	Polygon tool	Lets you draw polygons and stars.
	Basic shapes tool	Lets you choose from a full set of shapes, including hexagram, a smiley face, and a right-angle triangle.
	Text tool	Lets you type words directly on the screen as artistic text or a paragraph text.
	Interactive distortion tool	Lets you apply a Push or Pull distortion, a Zipper distortion, or a Twister distortion to an object.
	Eyedropper tool	Lets you select a fill from an object on the Drawing window.
	Outline tool	Opens a flyout that lets you set the outline properties.
	Fill tool	Opens a flyout that lets you set fill properties.
	Interactive fill tool	Lets you apply various fills.

Drawing Window

The Drawing window is the whole work area in the middle of your CorelDRAW 12 window, excluding the toolbars, toolbox (on the left), and status bar.

Note: The Drawing window is where you create graphics on the desktop.

Drawing Page

The section of the Drawing window bounded by the shaded box is called the Drawing page. This is the part of the composition that prints when you send a file to the printer.

You can store graphic images that you do not want to print (but do want to save) in the area of the Drawing window outside the Drawing page. The area outside the Drawing page can be a handy storage space when, for example, if you have a file that you use a template for a publication. You can save logos, blocks of text, etc. for use in another issue of your publication, but they would print if they are not on the Drawing page.

Property Bar

The Property Bar gives the information about any selected object in the Drawing window. The Property Bar changes, depending on what object you select in the Drawing window. There is a special Property Bar that appears when you do not have any object(s) selected. In Figure 1.4, because the Drawing window does not have any objects yet, the No selection Property Bar displays information about the Drawing page specification, such as page-size, etc.

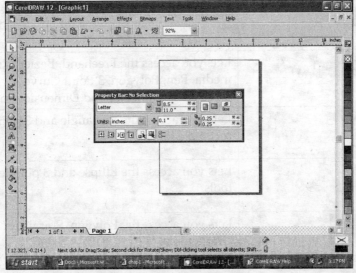

Figure 1.4 Property Bar

Note: The Property bar can float over the Drawing window. Moreover, you can dock it just below the Standard toolbar (or on either side or the bottom of Drawing window).

By default the Property Bar sits below the Standard toolbar but you can drag it on any portion of the Property Bar between tools or move it onto the Drawing window. If the Property bar is floating over the Drawing window, you can drag the Property Bar's title bar to move it as per your convenience. (See Figure 1.4)

Flyouts

Some tools have a small arrow in the lower left corner. If you click your cursor down on these tools, flyouts appear, and you can transform these tools into any other tools. These flyouts are explained in Table 1.3.

Table 1.3 Flyouts and their Description

Flyout	Description
Shape edit	Lets you access the Shape, Knife, Eraser, Smudge Brush, Roughen Brush, Free Transform and Virtual Segment delete tools
Zoom	Lets you access the Zoom and Pan tools
Curve	Lets you access the Freehand, Bezier, Artistic media, Pen, Polygon, 3 Point Curve, Interactive connector and Dimension tools.
Rectangle	Lets you access the Rectangle and 3 point rectangle tools
Ellipse	Lets you access the Ellipse and 3 point ellipse tools
Object	Lets you access the Polygon, Spiral and Graph tools
Perfect Shapes	Lets you access the Basic shapes, Arrow shapes, Flowchart shapes, Star shapes and Callout shapes tools.

Flyout	Description
Interactive tools	Lets you access the Interactive blend, Interactive contour, Interactive distortion, Interactive envelope, Interactive extrude, Interactive drop shadow and Interactive transparency tools.
Eyedropper tool	Lets you access the Eyedropper and Paintbucket tools.
Outline tool	Lets you access an Outline pen dialog, Outline color dialog, Color Docker window, Hairline Outline and a selection of outline of various widths.
Fill	Lets you access the Fill color, Fountain fill, Pattern fill, Texture fill, Postscript fill dialogs, and the Color Docker window.
Interactive tool	Lets you access Interactive fill and Interactive mesh tools.

Standard Toolbar

The Standard toolbar is directly under the Menu bar, and it displays icons for commands like New, Open, Save, Print, Copy, and Paste.

The Standard tools in toolbar are always available, but you can display additional tools as well.

Along with the Standard toolbar, CorelDRAW 12 activates interactive Property Bar when you select different types of objects. For example, if you select a shape, the Shape Property Bar appears under the Standard toolbar. If you select a text frame, the Text Property Bar becomes active. The elements of the Standard toolbar are explained in Table 1.4.

Table 1.4 Identifies the tools on the Standard toolbar.

Tool	Tool Name	What It Does?
	New	Opens a new file.

Tool	Tool Name	What It Does?
	Open	Activates the Open Drawing dialog box so you can open an existing file.
	Save	Resaved an already saved file, or opens the Save Drawing dialog box.
	Print	Print a drawing.
	Cut	Cuts selected objects and places them in the Clipboard, from which they can be pasted.
	Copy	Copies selected objects into the Clipboard.
	Paste	Pastes the contents of the Clipboard into the Drawing area.
	Undo	The icon undoes your last action; the drop-down list enables you to undo a series of actions.
	Redo	The icon redoes the last undone action; the drop-down list enables you to redo multiple undo actions.
	Import	Opens the Import dialog box from which you can import non-CorelDRAW files.
	Export	Opens the Export dialog box. Enabling you to export objects or files to other file formats.
51%	Zoom levels	The drop-down list enables you to zoom in or zoom out on your drawing
	Application Launcher	Enables you to start other CorelDRAW applications.
	Corel On'' ne	Opens your default Web browser and connects to Corel's online graphics Web site.

Note: Toolbars stay on the screen until you turn them off, and Property Bars appear or disappear depending on what objects you select.

Controlling the display of Toolbars

You can move toolbars onto the Drawing page, or dock them under the Standard toolbar. If you do not want the Property Bar to appear, right-click on it, and uncheck Property Bar from the context menu.

To control the display of Toolbars do this:

1. Right-click the Standard toolbar or the current Property Bar. A list of toolbars appears.

2. Click on the toolbar from the context menu you want to display. A toolbar is displayed when a check mark appears against the toolbar, as seen in Figure 1.5.

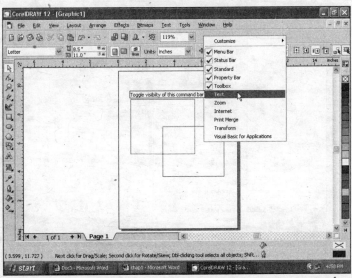

Figure 1.5 Checking text from Context Menu to display the text bar

Note: When you select to display the Text toolbar, it appears on your screen whether or not you have selected any text. Use this configuration if you are planning to do a lot of text editing and want the Text toolbar (or Property Bar, which is basically the same thing) always available.

To dock a toolbar do this:

1. Click the toolbar border, and drag the toolbar to the edge of the application window until it changes shape.

2. Release the mouse button to dock the toolbar.

To float a toolbar do this:

1. Click on a section of the toolbar between tools (not on a tool).

2. Drag the toolbar into the Drawing area.

Working with Docker Windows

Docker windows are similar to conventional dialog boxes, but are more interactive. They remain on the screen, until you close them. They can be placed next to the object you are drawing. This provides quick access to the commands placed in the docker window and their subsequent execution.

To see a list of Dockers available in the Dockers sub menu do this:

1. Click Windows menu, highlight Dockers as in Figure 1.6.

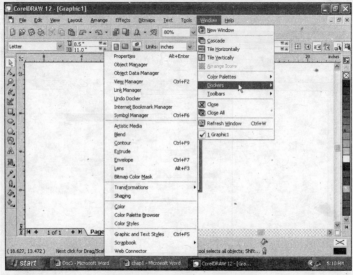

Figure 1.6 List of Dockers

In Figure 1.7, you see Transformation Dockers window available in CorelDRAW, which enables you to rotate the object. To introduce rotation of required degree you have to click the Apply button. The window does not disappear but sticks around. This helps you in experimenting with a series of rotations.

The Status Bar

The Status bar is located below the Drawing area and gives you important

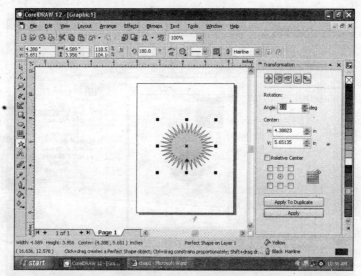

Figure 1.7 A Docker Window for applying rotation

information about a selected object. The status bar tells you the type of object you have selected and the type of fill. For example, in Figure 1.7, the status bar show that the object selected is a star and that the fill color is yellow. This is very useful when your illustration involves hundreds of objects. The status bar is a handy way to tell exactly what object is selected.

The status bar identifies the location of the cursor in x and y coordinates on the left side of the screen.

- The x value (the first one) represents the distance from the left edge of the Drawing page.
- The y value (the second one) represents the distance your current point is from the bottom of the Drawing page.

The Status bar also tells you what layer you are working with. (Complex Corel DRAW files can have more than one layer). (See Figure 1.8)

CorelDRAW View

You can control how you see and work with a page by selecting from five view options. CorelDRAW objects take quite a bit of system resources. When you fill a screen with objects, editing can be slow. Lower quality views can speed up that process. View quality settings from lowest to highest are:

- **Enhanced** It displays the drawing with postscript fills and high resolution.

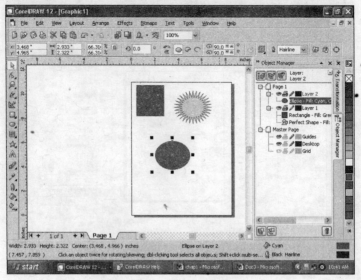

Figure 1.8 Status Bar elements

- **Normal** It displays the drawing without postscript fills and without high-resolution bitmapped images.
- **Draft** It displays a drawing's fills and bitmapped images using a low resolution.
- **Wireframe** It displays an outline of the drawing by hiding fills only.
- **Simple Wireframe** It displays an outline of the drawing by hiding fills, extrusions, contours, drop shadows, and intermediate blend shapes. It also displays the bitmapped images in monochrome.

Figures 1.9 to 1.13 shows the different views of the same drawing. The view you select affects the time it takes to open or refresh a drawing.

For example, a drawing in Simple Wireframe view opens or refreshes in less time than a drawing in enhanced view.

With CorelDRAW 12, enhanced view has become the default view setting. Enhanced view does provide a cleaner, less sharp picture of an illustration, but it is also slower to reflect drawing changes than Normal view. Depending on your PC hardware type and main memory in it, you can experiment by using Normal view. When you are working with pictures that slow your screen resolution, work in Draft view, and even Wireframe view if possible.

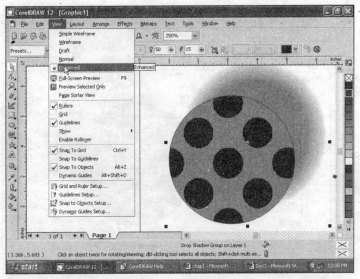

Figure 1.9 Enhanced view shows fills in high resolution

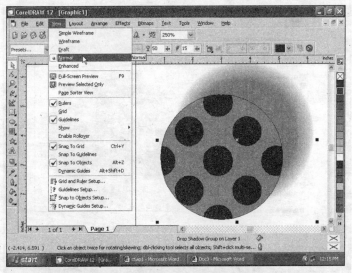

Figure 1.10 Normal view shows fills with low resolution.

Zooming and Panning

You can zoom in and out in CorelDRAW, and use the Pan tool to drag

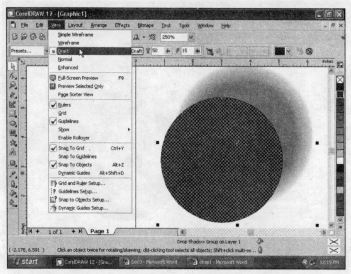

Figure 1.11 Draft view shows fill with low resolution

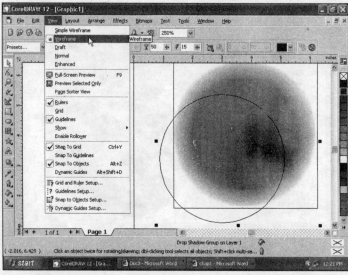

Figure 1.12 Wireframe view does not show the fills

parts of a drawing into the viewable window. The Zoom tool works as an interactive magnifying glass enabling you to focus on a small part of your page or zoom out to see the entire Drawing area. You can select different zoom magnifications.

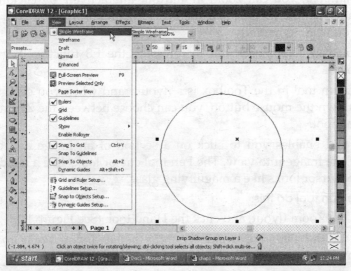

Figure 1.13   Simple Wireframe view hides the fills and dropshadows

To set different values of zoom do this:

1. Click the Zoom level from the Zoom Levels drop-down list in the Standard toolbar as in Figure 1.14.

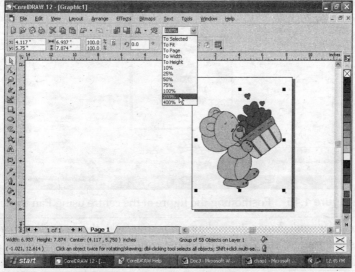

Figure 1.14   Zoom Levels in the Standard toolbar

2. *Alternatively*, you can zoom in and out interactively by clicking on the Zoom tool in the toolbox and then clicking on a portion of your drawing that you want to magnify.

3. Or you can Zoom back out by pressing the F3 function key on your keyboard.

4. The Zoom tool in the Toolbox is a flyout, and when you click on it and hold down the mouse button, you can choose between the Zoom tool and the Pan tool.

The Pan tool enables you to click on a section of an image and drag that section of the image into view. The Pan tool cursor looks like a hand, and the Zoom tool cursor looks like a magnifying glass.

To use the Pan tool do this:

1. Open the Zoom flyout, and click the Hand tool. (See Figure 1.15)

2. Drag in the Drawing window until the area you want to view is displayed.

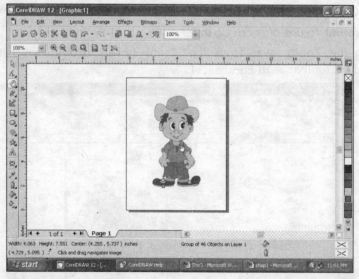

Figure 1.15   Positioning the figure at the centre using Pan tool

Note: The Pan and Zoom tools have no effect on the actual appearance of your finished image; they simply enable you to view images from different perspectives.

CHAPTER 2

Basic Drawing

Introduction

CorelDRAW 12 has different shape tools that you use to create lines, ellipses, circles, and rectangles including squares, polygons and stars. Shape tools have their own rules in CorelDRAW. In this chapter, you will learn to draw *lines*, *curves*, etc. using shape tools. Although CorelDRAW 12 has numerous effects and combinations of effects, most graphic designs boil down to combinations of shapes and text.

Working with Lines

Lines are the basic unit of almost all drawings. Therefore, you should first experiment with drawing lines before moving on to draw complex shapes.

CorelDRAW 12 lets you draw various different types of lines. These are *straight lines, freehand lines, calligraphic lines* and *Bezier lines.*

To draw a straight line, do this:

1. Click the **Curve** flyout from the toolbox, and choose the **Freehand** tool.
2. Click in the drawing window where you want to start the line. Now, click at a point, where you want to end it. A straight line will be formed joining these two points. (See Figure 2.1)
3. Using **Ctrl** key you can draw straight line angles in increments of 15°. That is you can draw straight lines at angles 0°, 15°, 30°, 45°, 60° and 90°, etc. This is useful for drawing *horizontal, vertical* and *straight* lines. After choosing the starting point, hold down **Ctrl** key. Now you will observe that the end point can be chosen only at the above particular angles. After pressing the **Ctrl** key, you cannot select end point at your will.

Drawing a Curve

CorelDRAW 12 gives you many options to draw curves. Freehand curve are the simplest of them all. Therefore, you will first learn to draw these.

Note: Freehand curve got its name because it looks much like a hand drawn curve.

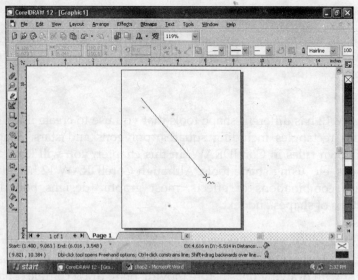

Figure 2.1   A straight line drawn using freehand tool.

To draw a freehand curve do this:

1. Click the Curve flyout, and choose the Freehand tool. Click and drag across the drawing page and draw a curve as you want it. (See Figure 2.2).

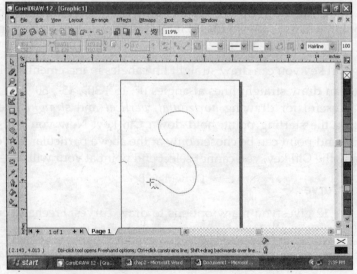

Figure 2.2   A curved line drawn with freehand curve tool

Bezier Lines and Curves

A line which is drawn one segment at a time by adding nodes are called Bezier lines. These lines can be drawn with the Bezier tool. Bezier lines and curves contain many nodes or control points. These nodes can be manipulated, dragged or pulled to draw the shape you want. Thus, the advantage with Bezier lines and curves lies in the fact that they can be modified after drawing them.

Note: Bezier curves are named after a French Engineer who developed the mathematical theory behind them in the 1970's.

To draw a Bezier line, do this:

1. Click the Curve flyout from the tool box, and choose the Bezier tool.
2. Click where you want to start the line, and go on clicking at points where you want to change the direction. (See Figure 2.3)

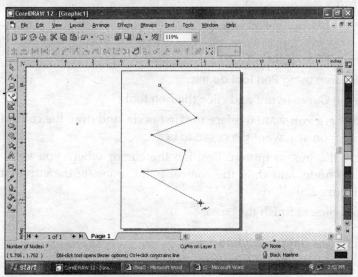

Figure 2.3   Drawing a Bezier line

To draw a Bezier curve do this:

1. Click the Curve flyout and choose Bezier tool.
2. Click at a point in the drawing window.
3. Then drag to shape the curve. Try to make a drawing, using Bezier tool, like the one shown in Figure 2.4.

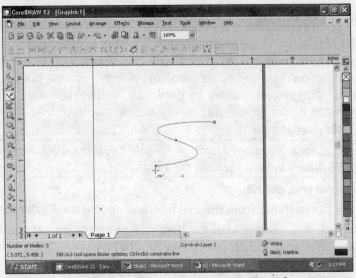

Figure 2.4 Bezier Curve drawn

Drawing Curve Using Pen Tool

To draw a curve using Pen tool do this:

1. Open the Curve flyout and click the Pen tool.
2. Click where you want to place the first node, and drag the control point in the direction you want the curve to bend.
3. Release the mouse button. Position the cursor where you want to place the next node, and drag the control point to create the curve you want. (See Figure 2.5)
4. Double-click to finish the curve.

Drawing Curve Using Polyline Tool

To draw a curve using Polyline tool do this:

1. Open the Curve flyout, and click the Polyline tool. Click where you want to start the curve, and drag across the drawing page. (See Figure 2.6)
2. Double-click to finish the curve

Drawing Curve Using 3-Point Curve Tool

To draw a curve using 3-Point Curve tool do this:

1. Open the Curve flyout, and click the 3 point curve tool.

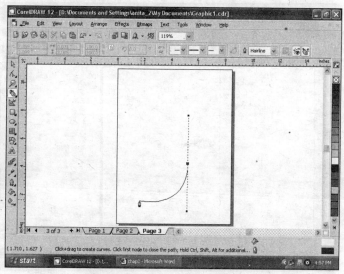

Figure 2.5   Curve using Pen tool

2. Click where you want to start the curve, and drag to where you want the curve to end.

3. Release the mouse button, and click where you want the center of the curve to be. (See Figure 2.7)

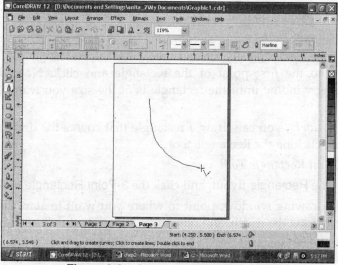

Figure 2.6   Curve using Polyline tool

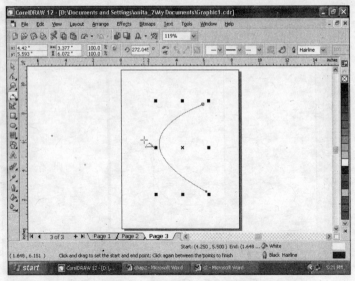

Figure 2.7 Curve using 3-Point Curve tool

Rectangles and Squares

Rectangles and squares are the basic shapes available with most drawing software packages. CorelDRAW 12 lets you draw rectangles and squares with great ease.

To draw a rectangle do this:

Using Rectangle Tool

1. Open the **Rectangle** flyout and then click the **Rectangle** tool. Move the cursor to the first point of the rectangle and click. Now drag in the drawing window until the rectangle is of the size you want. (See Figure 2.8)

2. *Alternatively*, you can draw a rectangle that covers the drawing page by double-clicking the Rectangle tool.

Using 3 Point Rectangle Tool

1. Open the **Rectangle** flyout, and click the **3-Point Rectangle** tool.

2. In the drawing window, point to where you want to start the rectangle, drag to draw the width, and release the mouse button. (See Figure 2.8)

3. Move the pointer to draw the height, and click.

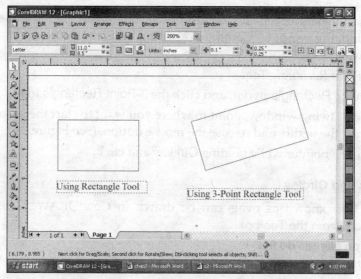

Figure 2.8 Different types of Rectangles

To draw a square do this:

Using Rectangle Tool

1. Open the **Rectangle** flyout and then click the **Rectangle** tool.

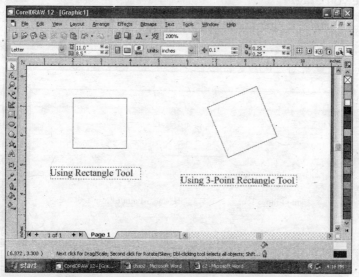

Figure 2.9 Different types of Squres

2. Press and hold down **Ctrl** key and drag diagonally the rectangle tool in the drawing window. Continue dragging until the Square is of the size you want. (See Figure 2.9).

Using 3 Point Rectangle Tool

1. Open the **Rectangle** flyout, and click the **3-Point Rectangle** tool.

2. In the drawing window, point to where you want to start the square, drag to draw the width, and release the mouse button. (See Figure 2.6)

3. Move the pointer while holding **Ctrl** key and click.

Ellipses and Circles

Ellipses also known as ovals can be drawn in CorelDRAW 12 using the *Ellipse* tool from the Toolbox.

To draw an ellipses do this:

Using Ellipse Tool

1. Open the **Ellipse** flyout, and click the **Ellipse** tool, and drag in the drawing window until the ellipse is the shape you want. (See Figure 2.10). The ellipse will continue to grow in size until you release the mouse button.

2. To draw an ellipse from the centre to outward, hold down the **Shift** key while you drag.

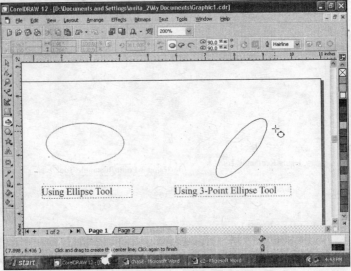

Figure 2.10 Different Types of Ellipse

Using 3 Point Ellipse Tool

1. Open the **Ellipse** flyout, and click the **3-Point Ellipse** tool.
2. In the drawing window, point to where you want to start the ellipse. Drag to draw the centerline, and release the mouse button. (See Figure 2.10)
3. Move the pointer to draw the height, and click.

To draw a circle do this:

Using Ellipse Tool

1. Open the **Ellipse** flyout, and click the **Ellipse** tool, press and hold down Ctrl key, and drag in the drawing window until the Circle is of the size you want. (See Figure 2.11)

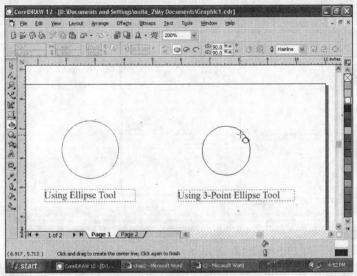

Figure 2.11 Different Types of Circles

2. To draw a circle from the centre to outward, hold down the **Ctrl + Shift** key together while you drag.

Using 3-Point Ellipse Tool

1. Open the **Ellipse** flyout, and click the **3-Point Ellipse** tool.
2. In the drawing window, point to where you want to start the circle, drag to draw the centerline, and release the mouse button. (See Figure 2.11)
3. Move the pointer while holding **Ctrl** key, and click.

Polygons and Stars

A Polygon is any closed figure with 3 or more sides. In CorelDRAW 12, you can draw polygons of any number of sides using the polygon tool. This tool also allows you to draw stars or polygon as stars.

To draw a polygons do this:

1. Click the **Object** flyout, choose the **Polygon** tool and drag in the drawing window until the polygon is of the size you want (See Figure 2.12). By default, the polygon drawn is a pentagon.

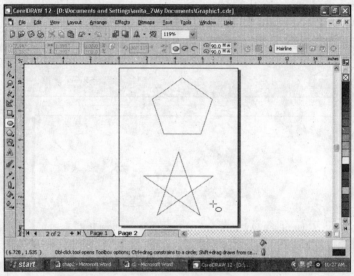

Figure 2.12 Drawing a Polygon and a Star

2. In order to draw polygons other than pentagon, type in the Property bar, the number of *points* or *sides* of the polygon which you want to create.

3. To draw a polygon from centre to outward hold down **Shift** key as you drag.

4. To draw a symmetrical polygon hold down **Ctrl** key as you drag.

To create a Star do this:

1. Click the **Object** flyout, choose **Polygon** tool, click the **Star** button on the property bar and then click and drag in the drawing window. (See Figure 2.12).

2. To draw a star from centre to outward, hold down **Shift** key as you drag.

3. To draw a symmetrical star press and hold down **Ctrl** key as you drag.

Selection Techniques

Before you can change an object, you must select it. You can select visible objects, hidden objects, and a single object in a group or a nested group. You can also select multiple objects all at once. You can also select objects in the order in which they were created.

To select objects do this:

1. Click **Pick** tool from the toolbox. Then click on the object with it. Or
2. To select many objects at once, hold down **Shift** key, and click each object you want to select. Or
3. To select all objects in the Drawing area, click the **Edit** menu and choose Select **All Objects**.
4. To select an object, starting with the first object created and moving toward the last object created, Press **Shift** + **Tab** keys together until a selection box displays around the object you want to select. Or
5. To select an object, starting with the last object created and moving toward the first object created, press **Tab** key until a selection box displays around the object you want to select.

To deselect already selected object(s) do this:

1. To deselect a single object click with the **Pick** tool a blank space in the drawing window.
2. To deselect a single object in multiple selected objects, press and hold down **Shift** key and click the object using the Pick tool.

Using Rulers

Rulers are the measuring tools displayed on the *left* side and along the *top* of the drawing window. The rulers help you size and position the objects in your drawing.

Rulers can help you *size*, *align* and *draw* objects accurately. You can hide the rulers or move them to another position in the drawing window. You can also customize the ruler settings to suit your needs. For example, you can set the ruler origin and select a unit of measure.

To control the display of rulers do this:

1. Click the **View** menu and choose **Rulers**. The ruler is displayed when a check mark appears.
2. To hide the ruler click again.

When you move any object, you can see a white dotted line on the left and top rulers. These lines help you to position your object correctly.

To customize ruler settings do this:

1. Click <u>V</u>iew menu and choose Grid and Ru<u>l</u>er Setup... . You will find that Option Dialog box appears.

2. In Option dialog box, in the list of categories, click Rulers in the options dialog box as seen in Figure 2.13. *Alternatively*, the options dialog box can also be opened by double clicking anywhere on the rulers.

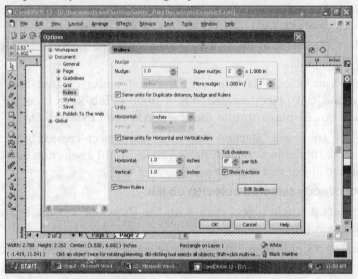

Figure 2.13 Rulers dialog box with Options

3. The Nudge: This specifies how far the object moves when you press up, down, right or left arrow key. For example, if you set Nudge to 1 inch and choose the object using Pick tool, then if you press down arrow key, the object will move 1 inch down.

4. To set units of measurements for the placement of duplicate objects and nudge values different from that of ruler units, uncheck the Same units for Duplicate distance, Nudge (move an object in increment) and Rulers check box.

Note: Duplicate objects are created by pressing Ctrl+D *keys together. Alternatively, duplicate objects can be created by clicking* <u>E</u>dit *menu and then choosing* <u>D</u>uplicate.

5. In the Units area, choose a unit of measure from the Horizontal: list box.

6. To set different units of measurements for the Vertical and Horizontal rulers, uncheck the Same units for Horizontal and Vertical rulers check box, and then type the values in the Horizontal: and Vertical: list box.

7. In the Origin area, type values for the origin in the Horizontal: and Vertical: list box.

8. To divide a unit into a fixed number of sub divisions other than the default value, type a value in the Tick divisions box.

9. Uncheck or check Show Rulers check box to show/hide rulers.

To move rulers do this:

1. Hold down Shift Key

2. Drag the rulers to the desired position

Using Grids and Guidelines

Grids and guidelines are tools that enable you to easily position a selected object to a horizontal or vertical location, or both.

Working with the grid displayed is like working on graph paper. You can use grids to align an object to a position. The grids are not printed. Similarly, guidelines are non-printing lines placed to align and place the objects in your drawing. Guidelines are of two types, vertical and horizontal. Figure 2.14 shows a horizontal and a vertical guidelines.

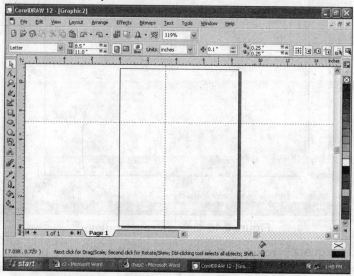

Figure 2.14 A horizontal and vertical guidelines

Snap to Grid feature will make the grid coordinates act like magnets that attract the object you are moving. If you want to move an object to a location not on a grid coordinate, you will find it difficult with Snap to Grid turned on.

Finally, you can place custom-defined horizontal and vertical guidelines on your page and use them to align objects to a required position.

Note: The hotkey for toggling Snap to Grid on and off is Ctrl+Y.

Defining Grids

To display grids do this:

1. Click Ⅴiew menu and choose Ⅾrid.
2. You can also adjust the distance between the grids. Also the frequency, i.e. the number of lines between each vertical and horizontal unit, can be set according to your requirement. The intersecting horizontal and vertical lines are called gridlines.

To customize grids do this:

1. Click Ⅴiew menu and choose Grid and Ruler Setup. The Option dialog box appears as in Figure 2.15.

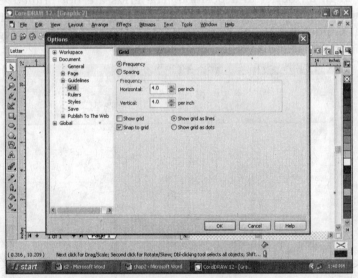

Figure 2.15 Customizing Gridlines

2. Click Frequency radio button, to specify the number of lines per unit measurement and indicate the frequency for Horizontal and Vertical grid.

3. Click Spacing radio button, to specify the distance between each grid line. Type values in the following boxes.

   In the Horizontal: list box type the distance between horizontal grid.

   In the Vertical: list box type the distance between vertical grid.

4. To display the girds as lines, click the Show grid as line radio button.

5. To display the grids as dots, click the Show gird as dots radio button.

6. To display the grid click Show grid check box.

Note: While customizing guides you have two options. Specify the guides by specifying the frequency in the selection or specify the spacing between the grids.

Snap to Grid

You can also have objects snap to gridlines so that when they are moved they jump between the nearest grid line or dot.

To get objects snap to grid do this:

1. Click View menu and choose Snap To Grid or press Ctrl+Y keys together.

Defining Guidelines

To place a Horizontal or Vertical Guideline, do this:

1. Drag on the ruler (on the left side for vertical guideline or top for horizontal guideline) of the Drawing window, and pull it to the position you want to place the guide.

2. *Alternatively*, Click View menu and choose Guidelines Setup.... The dialog box appears as in Figure 2.16.

3. In the dialog box, click the Vertical or Horizontal as per your need.

4. Specify the setting you want.

5. Click Add button.

Snap to Guidelines

Snap to guidelines features, when turned on, makes the guidelines behave like magnets. That is when you move the object near the guidelines it sticks to the guideline.

To snap to guidelines do this:

1. Click on View menu and choose Snap to Guidelines. Now the guidelines will act as magnetic borders.

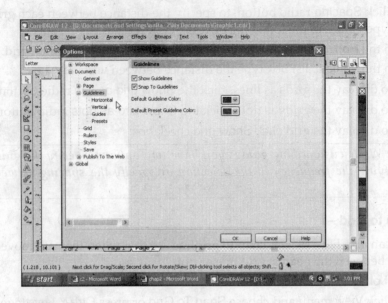

Figure 2.16 Setting up guideline through the dialog box

To remove guidelines do this:

1. Select the guideline you want to remove with the Pick tool.
2. Press the Delete button.

CorelDRAW 12 allows you to snap the objects. That is, you can force an object that is being drawn to align automatically to a point on another object.

Snap to Objects

Snap to object means to force an object to align automatically to a point on the grid, a guideline, or another object. You can snap an object to a number of snap points in the target object. When the pointer is close to a snap point, the snap point is highlighted, indicating it as the target that the pointer will snap to. For example, you can snap the pointer to a rectangle's center, and then drag the rectangle by its center and snap it to the center of another rectangle.

To customize snap to objects do this:

1. Click on Yiew menu and choose Snap to Objects Setup... . The dialog box appears as seen in Figure 2.17.
2. In the *Snapping modes* area, enable one or more of the mode check boxes.
3. If you want to enable all snapping modes, click Select all.

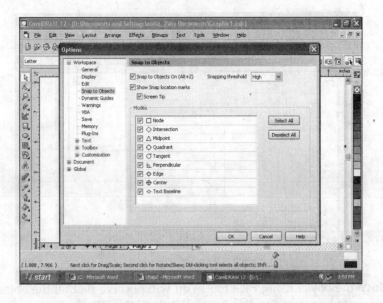

Figure 2.17 Customizing Snapping Objects

4. If you want to disable all snapping modes, but without turning off snapping, click **Deselect all**.

5. Display or hide snapping mode indicators, Enable or disable the **Show snap location marks** check box.

6. Display or hide screen tips, Enable or disable the **Screen tip** check box.

7. Choose one of the following snapping options from the Snapping threshold list box:

   Low: This activates a snap point when it is four pixels away from the pointer.

   Medium: This activates a snap point when it is eight pixels away from the pointer.

   High: This activates a snap point when it is sixteen pixels away from the pointer.

To snap to Objects do this:

1. Select the objects.

2. Click <u>V</u>iew and choose **Snap To Objects**. Or Alternatively Click **Ctrl + Z** keys together. (See Figure 2.18)

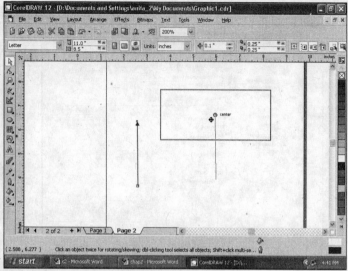

3. Move the object using **Pick** tool. You will observe that all the objects will appear to be magnetized and stick tightly to the other object.

Figure 2.18 Snap Arrow to Rectangle

Using Dynamic Guides

Dynamic guides help you to precisely move, align, and draw objects relative to other objects. These guides are temporary guidelines that you can pull from the following snap points in objects — center, node, quadrant, and text baseline.

When you drag an object along a dynamic guide, you can view the object's distance from the snap point used to create the dynamic guide, and place the object precisely. The screen tip displays the angle of the dynamic guide and the distance between the node and the pointer. Dynamic guides contain invisible divisions called ticks to which your pointer moves. Ticks let you move objects with precision along a dynamic guide. You can also set other options for dynamic guides. For example, you can choose to display dynamic guides at one or more preset angles, or at custom angles you specify.

To display dynamic guides do this:

1. Click <u>V</u>iew and choose **Dynamic Guides**. Or *Alternatively* Click **Alt + Shift + D** keys together.

2. Click on a drawing tool which you create.

3. Move the pointer over and then off an eligible snap point of an object.

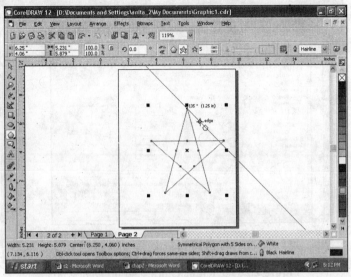

Figure 2.19 Dynamic Guides

4. Repeat step 3 with other objects to display other dynamic guides.

5. The snap points you point to are registered in a queue and are used to create dynamic guides. (See Figure 2.19)

Note: To avoid displaying too many dynamic guides, you can clear the queue of points at any time by pressing Esc key.

To customize dynamic guide options do this:

1. Click <u>V</u>iew and choose Dynamic Guides Setup... . The dialog box appears as shown in Figure 2.20.

2. Click on Angle screen tip check box to display or hide the angle of dynamic guides

3. Click on Distance check box to display or hide the distance from the snap point.

4. Type a value in the Tick spacing box to change the distance between the invisible divisions on the dynamic guides.

5. In the Guides area, enable or disable the angle check boxes to choose the angles at which to create the dynamic guides.

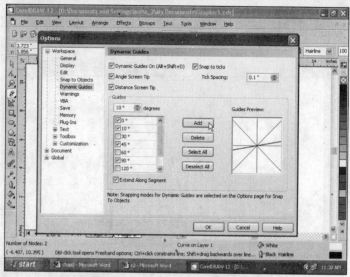

Figure 2.20 Dynamic Guides Set up Dialog box

6. In the Guides area, type a value in the **Degrees** box, and click **Add** to display a custom dynamic guide by specifying its angle.

7. To delete a particular angle setting click on **Delete** button.

8. To select all angles given in Guides area **Select All** button.

9. If you do not want to show the dynamic guides on the predefined angles you can deselect them by pressing **Deselect All** button.

10. Enable the **Extend along segment** check box to create dynamic guides that are extension of line segments.

Spirals and Graphs

With CorelDRAW you can draw spiral shapes and graphs.

Spirals

To draw spirals, do this:

1. Click the **Object** flyout and choose **Spiral** tool.

2. Specify the number of revolutions you want in the **Spiral Revolutions** list box.

3. Click and drag in the drawing window till the spiral is of the desired size. (See Figure 2.21)

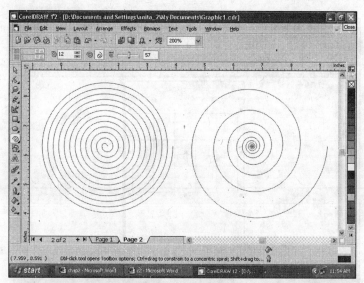

Figure 2.21 A symmetrical (left) logarithmic (right) spirals

4. If you don't want the spiral to be symmetrical, click on the **Logarithmic Spiral** button in the property bar.

5. Set the **spiral expansion factor** by dragging the slider on the property bar.

Note: You can draw a spiral from its center outward by holding down **Shift** *key as you drag. You can also draw a spiral with even horizontal and vertical dimensions by holding down* **Ctrl** *key as you drag.*

Graphs

To draw graph, do this:

1. Click the **Object** flyout and choose **Graph Paper** tool

2. Click and drag in the drawing window till the graph is of the desired size is formed. (See Figure 2.22)

3. You can set the number of rows and columns in the Graph Paper Rows and Columns list box in the property bar. The top box specifies the number of columns and the bottom box specifies the number of rows.

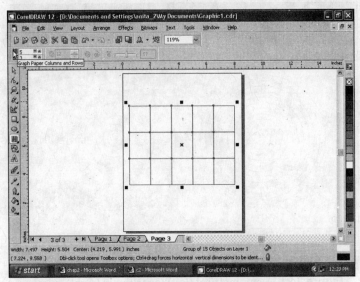

Figure 2.22 A graph with 3 rows and 5 columns drawn using
the Graph Paper tool

CHAPTER 3

Artistic Media Tool

Introduction

The Artistic media tool is used to draw curves like the Freehand tool. As in Freehand tool, Artistic media tool also draws a curve by clicking and then dragging.

Artistic Media tool is actually a collection of many tools. Each tool has its own settings and effects. When you click on the Artistic media tool in the Curve flyout, the property bar displays these different tools. When you click on a tool, the corresponding settings and effects are displayed on the property bar (See Figure 3.1).

Using Preset Tool

Preset line is the name given to thick lines that can be drawn in CorelDRAW 12 using the preset button. These lines can be drawn of different shapes according to the requirement.

CorelDRAW provides you certain preset lines that can be chosen to draw lines of your choice.

To draw a line using preset tool, do this:

1. Click the Curve flyout and choose the Artistic media tool.
2. Click the Preset button on the Property bar.120
3. Choose a preset line shape from the Preset stroke list box. (See Figure 3.1) It shows the property bar displayed when Preset button is clicked.

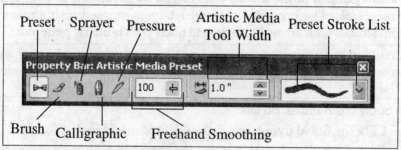

Figure 3.1   Property Bar for Artistic Media Preset Tool.

4. If you want to smoothen the edges of the line, type a value in the Freehand Smoothing box on the property bar.

5. If you want to set the width of the line, type a value in the Artistic media tool width box on the property bar.

6. Click on the Preset drop down menu and choose a preset line.

7. Drag on the Drawing window with a mouse to shape the curve you want. You can apply fills also to these preset lines (See Figure 3.2).

Figure 3.2 A Line Drawn Using Preset tool.

Using Brush Tool

With CorelDRAW, you can apply a variety of preset brush strokes. The width and smoothness of the brushstroke can be set according to your choice. The Brush Stroke List drop down menu lets you choose brush strokes ranging from strokes with arrow heads to one filled with rainbow patterns.

Note: You can also create custom brush strokes using an object or a group of vector objects. When you create a custom brush stroke, you can save it as a preset

To apply brush stroke, do this:

1. Click the Curve flyout, and choose Artistic media tool.

2. Click on the Brush button in the Property bar. Figure 3.3 shows the Brush Stroke Property bar.

3. Choose a brush stroke from the Brush stroke list box.

4. To smoothen the edges of the stroke, type a value in the Freehand smoothing box on the property bar.

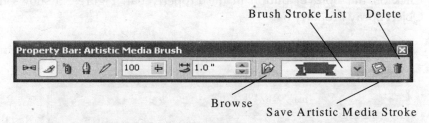

Figure 3.3 Artistic Media Brush Property Bar.

5. To set the width, type a value in the **Artistic media tool width** box on the Property bar.

6. Drag on the Drawing window to shape your stroke (See Figure 3.4).

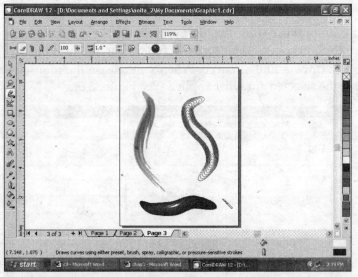

Figure 3.4 Different types of Brush Strokes

Note: If a brush stroke is not listed in the **Brush stroke** *list box, you can locate the brush stroke file by clicking the* **Browse** *button on the property bar.*

Using Object Sprayer Tool

The Object Sprayer tool provides effects that look nothing at all like the line you will draw.

To apply Sprayer tool effects, do this:

1. Click the **Curve** flyout and choose the **Artistic media** tool.

2. Click on the **Sprayer** button in the Property bar. Figure 3.5 shows the Object Spray Property bar.

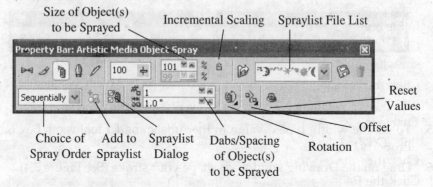

Size of Object(s) to be Sprayed — Incremental Scaling — Spraylist File List

Reset Values

Offset

Choice of Spray Order — Add to Spraylist — Spraylist Dialog — Dabs/Spacing of Object(s) to be Sprayed — Rotation

Figure 3.5   The Object Spray Property Bar

3. Choose a spraylist from the **Spraylist file list** box. Click on the **Browse** button to choose a different spraylist other than that listed in the list box.

4. Drag and draw a line or curve. When you release the mouse button, you will see the selected spraylist applied (See Figure 3.6).

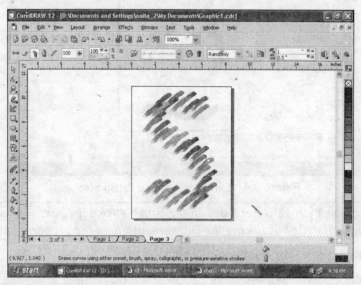

Figure 3.6   The Blue Brush Strokes are Spray Objects drawn as a Curve.

5. To set the spray order, choose a spray order from the Choice of spray order list box.

6. In the Size of objects to be sprayed box, set the size of spray objects,.

7. In the top box of the Dabs/Spacing of objects to be sprayed box, type a value, to adjust the number of objects sprayed at each point. Type a value in the bottom box to set the spacing between dabs.

8. Click the Reset values button, to undo these settings and reset the spraylist to its default settings.

9. Click the Rotation button, to rotate a line. In the Angle box, type a value for rotation.

   Enable the Use Increment check box to rotate each object in the spray and type a value for increment in the Increment box, to rotate step by step.

   Click the Path based radio button, to rotate objects in relation to line.

   Click the Page based radio button and Press Enter key, to rotate objects in relation to page.

Using spray objects, you can create a variety of wonderful drawings. The drawing in Figure 3.7 has been drawn using just spray objects.

Figure 3.7   This Figure is drawn using Object Sprayer

Using Calligraphic Tool

Calligraphic lines are similar to lines drawn using a calligraphic pen. Such lines change their thickness according to the direction of the line. Line's thickness also varies depending upon the angle of the pen nib.

To draw a Calligraphic line or curve, do this:

1. Click the Curve flyout and choose the Artistic media tool.
2. Click the Calligraphic button on the Property bar. Figure 3.8 shows the Property bar for calligraphic button.

Calligraphic Angle

Figure 3.8 The Artistic Media Calligraphic Property Bar

3. Type a value in the Calligraphic angle box on the Property bar.
4. If you want to smoothen the edges of the line, type a value in the Freehand Smoothing box on the Property bar. If Property bar is not visible, right click the tool in the toolbox, and check Property bar.
5. Drag until the line is the shape you want.
6. To set the width of the line, type a value in the Artistic media tool width box on the Property bar. Figure 3.9 shows a Calligraphic curved line.

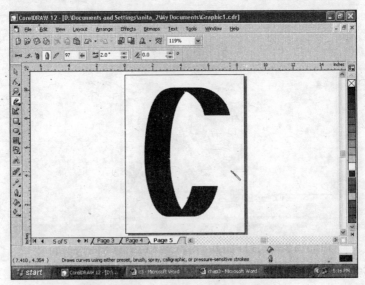

Figure 3.9 Calligraphic Curved Line

Pressure-Sensitive Lines or Curves

Pressure sensitive lines are those lines with curved edges that vary in width or thickness along a path. This effect can be created using mouse or a pressure-sensitive pen.

To draw a pressure sensitive line or curve, do this:

1. Click the Curve flyout and choose Artistic media tool.
2. Click the Pressure button on the Property bar. Figure 3.10 shows the property bar for the pressure sensitive line.

Freehand Smoothing   Artistic Media Tool Width

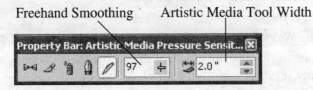

Figure 3.10 The Artistic Media Pressure Sensitive Pen Property Bar

3. To smooth the edges of the line, type a value in the Freehand smoothing box on the Property bar.
4. To change the width of the line, type a value in the Artistic media tool width box on the Property bar.
5. Drag until the line is the shape you want. Figure 3.11 shows a pressure-sensitive line.

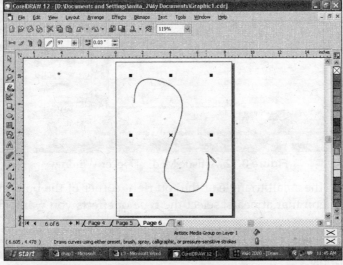

Figure 3.11 Drawing a Pressure Sensitive Curve

Applying Artistic Media Effects

Till now, you were selecting the Artistic media effects that you needed from the Property bar. After selecting the desired effect you would drag and draw a curve in the drawing window. The selected effect gets applied to the curve. But by using the Artistic media docker window, you can apply changes to a curve, interactively. You can apply the desired artistic effect to an already drawn simple curve. You can also replace an artistic media effect with another effect, which is not possible with property bar.

To use Artistic Media docker window, do this:

1. Draw any curve.
2. Click on the Window menu, highlight Dockers and choose Artistic Media.
3. The top part of the Docker window shows the list of Artistic media tools you recently used. The bottom part of the window shows the effects (See Figure 3.12).

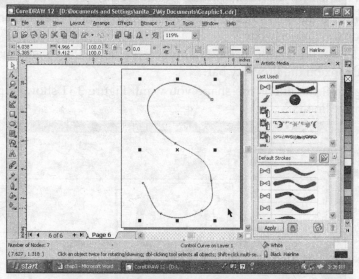

Figure 3.12 Artistic Media Docker Window

4. Click on the small triangle at the top right corner of the bottom window. In the menu that appears, select the type of effects you want. (See Figure 3.13)
5. Choose an effect from the Docker window.
6. Click Apply.

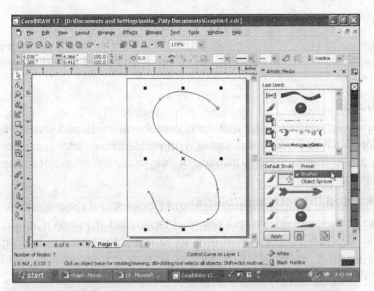

Figure 3.13 Choosing Type of Effect from the Docker Window

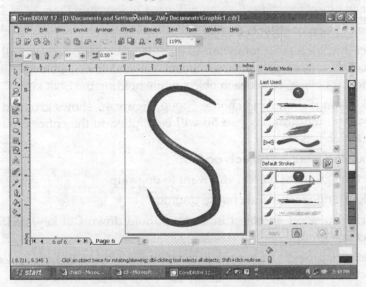

Figure 3.14 Clicking the brush stroke type from the styles

CHAPTER 4

Advanced Drawing

Introduction

In Chapter 3, you learnt to work with the basic tools and shapes available with CorelDRAW 12. In this Chapter, you will learn advance concepts used in drawings and managing the drawing objects using technique of grouping and ungrouping.

Grouping and Ungrouping Objects

A group is the name given to a set of objects that behave as a single unit on selection. Operations performed on a group of objects are applied equally to all the objects. A nested group is a group of two or more groups that behaves as a single object.

Note: Once objects are grouped, you cannot work on individual objects. To work on an object individually, you will need to ungroup them.

To create a group of objects do this:

1. Select the objects that you want to include in a group. To select all objects, click Edit menu and choose Select All and then Objects. To select particular objects, select each object while holding the Shift key.
2. Click Arrange menu and choose Group. Figure 4.1 shows grouped objects. Now any modifications you do will be applied to the entire group of the selected objects.

To ungroup the grouped objects do this:

1. Select the group of objects you want to ungroup.
2. Click Arrange menu and choose Ungroup.
3. In order to select an object in a group, hold down Ctrl key, and click an object in a group.
4. To select an object in a nested group, hold down Ctrl key, and click an object you want to select until a selection box displays around it.

Note: You can also select one or more objects by dragging around the object.

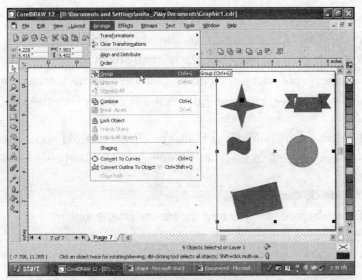

Figure 4.1   Grouping the objects

In the following section you will learn to use the various editing tools in CorelDRAW 12. These tools are located in the **Shape Edit** flyout (See Figure 4.2) and their usage is discussed in the following sections.

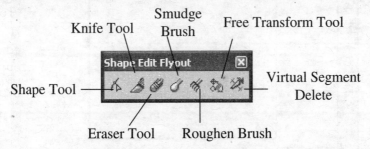

Figure 4.2   The Shape Edit flyout.

Editing Curves with Nodes

The small square points at the end of a line or a curve segment are called nodes. These nodes can be dragged or pulled anywhere to change the shape of a line, curve or other shapes.

To select or deselect node(s) from the object do this:

1. Click the **Shape edit** flyout, and choose the **Shape** tool in the Property tool box.

2. Select the object for which you want to edit the nodes.

3. Click a node on the curve object i.e. a small box in the object.

4. To select multiple nodes, hold down **Shift** key, and click each node.

5. To select all nodes, click the **Edit** menu, highlight **Select All** and choose **Nodes**.

6. To deselect a node hold down **Shift**, and click a selected node.

7. To deselect multiple nodes, hold down **Shift** key, and click each selected node.

To add a node do this:

1. Click the **Shape edit flyout** and choose the **Shape tool**.

2. Select the curve object, and double-click where you want to add a node as seen in Figure 4.3.

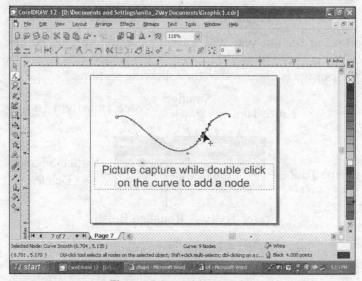

Figure 4.3 Adding nodes

To delete a node do this:

1. Click the **Shape edit flyout** and choose the **Shape tool**.

2. Select the curve object, and double-click the node which you want to delete.

To rotate and skew nodes do this:

1. Click the **Shape edit** flyout and choose the **Shape** tool.
2. Select a curve object.
3. Select the nodes along the curve which you want to transform.
4. From the Property bar, choose **Stretch and scale nodes** or **Rotate and skew nodes** (See Figure 4.4)
5. Drag a set of handles to transform the nodes.

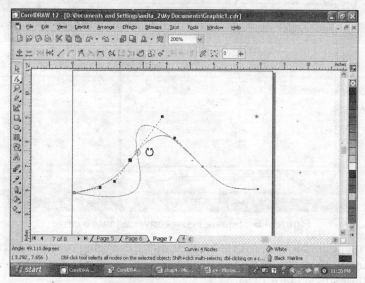

Figure 4.4   Rotating nodes

Editing Shapes using Nodes

Like curves we can also edit other shapes such as *ellipses, rectangles* or *polygons*.

To edit shapes do this:

1. Click the **Shape edit** flyout and choose the **Shape** tool.
2. Click the shape you want to edit with this tool.
3. Nodes will appear (See Figure 4.4). Move these nodes to change the shape of the rectangle, polygon or ellipse.
   - Edges of rectangle become rounded when one of the nodes along the outline of the rectangle is dragged.

- Square can be converted into a circle with the help of nodes. Drag any of the four nodes situated at the corners. Drag the node to the Rounded rectangle edges and the square will be converted into a circle. (See Figure 4.5)

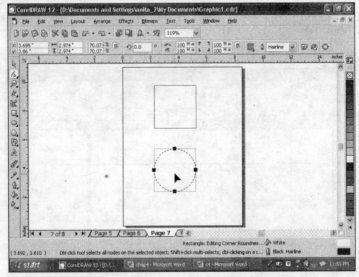

Figure 4.5 Square being converted into a circle

- Polygons can be converted into stars by dragging on the side or corner nodes (See Figure 4.6). And a star can be converted into a fan like figure. (See Figure 4.7)

4. Ellipses and circles have only a single node. This node can be dragged with the Shape tool to create an arc or pie (See Figure 4.8).

Note: When you click and drag any of the nodes on a shape, the effect is applied to all the nodes. If you wish to work on individual nodes you will have to convert the shape into curve.

To edit individual nodes, do this:

1. Select the shape.
2. Click Arrange menu and choose Convert to curves.
3. *Alternatively,* you can click on the Convert To curve button on the property bar.

You can now drag and modify each node as you like.

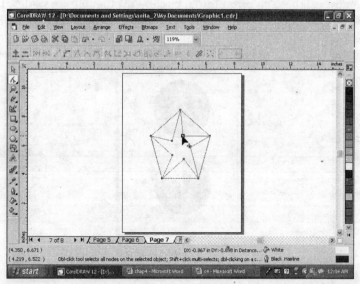

Figure 4.6   Polygon being converted into a star by dragging node

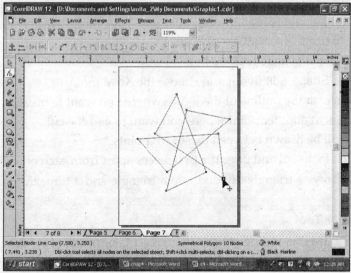

Figure 4.7   5-point star being converted using shape tool

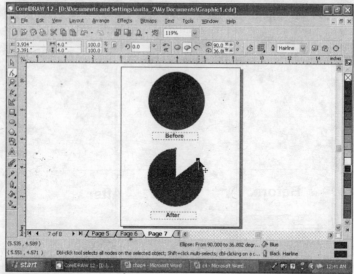

Figure 4.8   By dragging the node, the circle is made into pie-slice shapes

Using Knife Tool

The knife tool as the name indicates cuts the object into pieces. You will now learn how to use this tool to cut drawings.

To edit drawing with knife tool, do this:

1. Click the Shape edit flyout and choose the Knife tool.
2. Click once on the outline of the figure where you want to break.
3. Then click at another point where you want to end the cut.
4. A line will be drawn between these two points.
5. Click the Pick tool and drag the two pieces apart from each other.

Figure 4.9 shows a triangle divided into a triangle and a trapezium using the knife tool.

Using Eraser Tool

Eraser tool is used to remove the unwanted parts or pixels of an object. Eraser tool is also used to draw white drawings on black background.

To erase a part of a drawing do this:

1. Select the object on which you want to use the Eraser tool.
2. Click the Shape edit flyout and choose the Eraser tool.

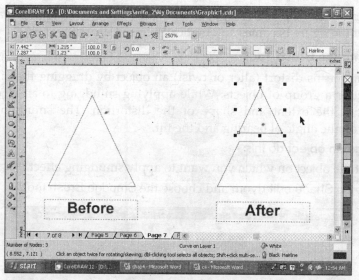

Figure 4.9   Triangle is divided into a triangle and a trapezium with knife tool

3. Drag Eraser on the line which you do not want (See Figure 4.10).

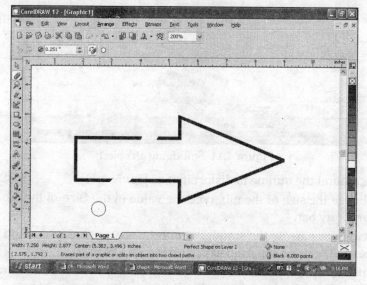

Figure 4.10 The arrow line being erased with the Eraser tool

4. Observe that the pixels disappear and when you stop dragging Eraser, the rest of the figure becomes automatically closed up.

Using Smudge Brush Tool

Smudging means distort (alter or twist) an object by dragging the outline of the object or a group of objects. While applying smudging to an object, you can control the extent and shape of the distortion. The smudging effect depends on the angle of bearing and the tilt.

To smudge an object do this:

5. Select the object on which you want to apply smudging effect.
6. Click the Shape edit flyout and choose the Smudge Brush tool.

Figure 4.11 Smudging an object

7. Drag around the outline to distort it. (See Figure 4.11)
8. To change the size of the nib, type the value in the Size of the nib box on the property bar.
9. To widen or narrow the smudging effect, type a value in the Add dry out to the effect box on the property bar between –10 to 10.
10. To specify the shape of the smudging, type a value between 1 and 90 in the Enter a fixed value for tilt settings box on the property bar.

11. To specify the angle of the nib shape for smudging, type a value in the **Enter a fixed value for bearing setting** box on the property bar.

Note: To smudge the inside of an object, click outside of an object and drag inwards. To smudge the outside of an object, click inside of an object and drag outwards.

Using Roughen Brush Tool

The Roughen Brush tool applies a jagged or spiked edge to objects, including lines, curves, and text. You can control the size, angle, direction, and number of the indentations.

To roughen an object

1. Select an object using the Pick tool.
2. Open the **Shape edit** flyout, and click the **Roughen Brush** tool.
3. Point to the area on the outline you want to roughen, and drag the outline to distort it. (See Figure 4.12)

Figure 4.12 Left object after applying rough brush, left object during roughening

4. To specify the size of the roughening spikes, type a value in the **Size of the nib** box on the property bar.
5. To change the number of spikes in a roughened area, type a value between 1 and 10 in the **Enter a value for frequency of spikes** box on the property bar.

6. To specify the height of the roughening spikes, Type a value between 1 and 90 in the Enter a fixed value for tilt settings box on the property bar.

7. To increase/decrease the number of roughening spikes, type a value in the Add dry out to the effect box on the property bar.

8. To specify the direction of the roughening spikes Choose from the Spike direction list box.

9. Type a value between 0 and 359 in the Enter a fixed value for bearing settings box on the property bar.

Using Free Transform Tool

Using the free transform tool of the Shape edit flyout, you can transform the shape of any figure along a particular node.

To transform a drawing using free transform tool, do this:

1. Click on the Shape Edit flyout and choose the Free Transform tool.

2. To rotate the figure along a node choose Free Rotation button from the property bar. Then click on any node and drag to a point. You will see that the object pivots on that node (See Figure 4.13).

Figure 4.13 A Gardener's picture has been pivoted using the Free Rotation tool

3. Free Angle Reflection button creates a mirror image of the object in the angle you define (See Figure 4.14).

Figure 4.14 Picture of the woman has been mirror reflected using the Angle Reflection tool

4. The Free Scaling button on the property bar can be used to change the horizontal and vertical length of the object (See Figure 4.15).

Figure 4.15 The image has been scaled to a larger size than its original size

5. Free Skewing button changes the shape of the object when a node is dragged (See Figure 4.16).

Figure 4.16 Image skewed using the Free Skew tool

Using Virtual Segment Delete Tool

With the help of Virtual Segment delete tool, you can delete portions of objects, (called virtual line segments) that are between intersections.

To delete a portion of the object or a ine segment do this:

1. Open the Shape edit flyout, and click the Virtual Segment Delete tool.
2. Move the pointer to the line segment and then click the line segment. (See Figure 4.17)
3. If you want to delete multiple line segments at one time, click the pointer to drag a marquee around all line segments you want to delete.

Note: The Virtual segment delete *tool sudden move upright when positioned properly and it does not work on linked groups.*

Drawing using Shape Recognition (Smart Drawing Tool)

CorelDRAW 12 provide you a facility to draw freehand strokes that are recognized and converted to basic shapes using the **Smart drawing** tool. It automatically smoothes any unrecognized shapes or curves drawn with the

Smart drawing tool. If an object is not converted to a shape, it can be beautified. Objects and curves drawn with shape recognition are editable.

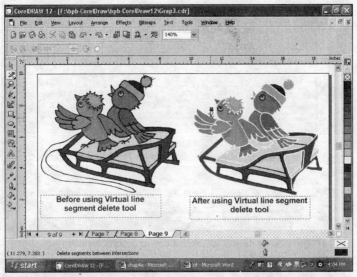

Figure 4.17 Virtual segment delete tool deletes the line segment

To draw a shape using smart drawing tool do this:

1. Click the Smart drawing tool from the tool box.

2. Choose a level of recognize an object from the Recognition level list box on the property bar.

3. Choose a level of smoothing an object from the Smoothing level list box on the property bar.

4. Draw a shape in the drawing window. (See Figure 4.18)

Example

Now that you have learned the methods to transform object shapes, let us create a drawing shown in Figure 4.19 using simple shapes.

To transform basic drawings that you learnt so far, into the sail boat, do this:

Steps to draw the sail

1. Click the Polygon tool from the toolbox. In the property bar type 3 for number of sides.

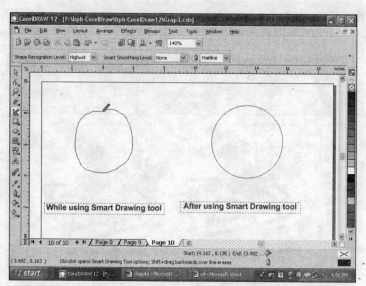

Figure 4.18 Draw an object using Smart Drawing tool

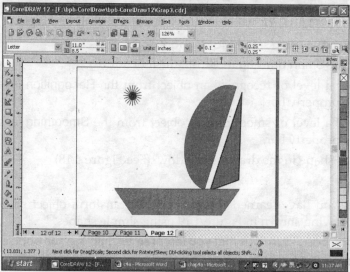

Figure 4.19 A sail boa made using simple shapes.

2. Drag in the drawing window. A triangle will be formed (See Figure 4.20).

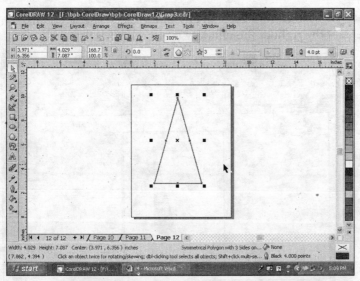

Figure 4.20 Triangle drawn using polygon tool.

3. Click the **Knife** tool from the **Shape Edit** flyout. Divide the triangle into two triangles as seen in Figure 4.21. Delete the left triangle.

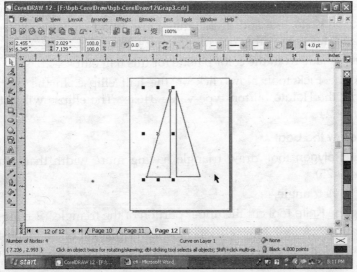

Figure 4.21 The selected half of the triangle to be deleted

4. Select the triangle and click on any of the black shade you like on the color Palette at the right of the window (See Figure 4.22).

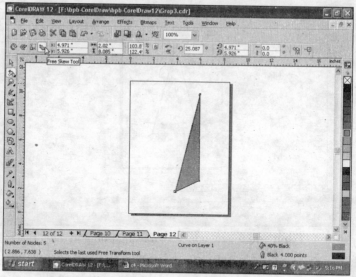

Figure 4.22 Triangle skewed and shaded.

5. Click the **Ellipse** tool and draw an ellipse on the Drawing area.
6. Click the **Knife** tool and divide the ellipse into two halves. Keep the left half and delete the other one (See Figure 4.23).
7. Select a shade from the color palette for this half ellipse.
8. Click the **Pick** tool. Now click on the half ellipse. In the property bar against the **Rotate** button type value 346.6°. The ellipse will rotate as in Figure 4.24.

Steps to draw the boat

1. Using **Polygon** tool, draw triangle having more width than height (See Figure 4.25).
2. Select this triangle.
3. Using the **Knife** tool cut the upper portion of the triangle. (See Figure 4.26)
4. Click the **Pick** tool. Now click on the lower portion of the triangle. In the property bar against the rotate button type value 180°. The ellipse will rotate as in Figure 4.27.
5. Click and choose a shade for the base of sail boat from the color palette.

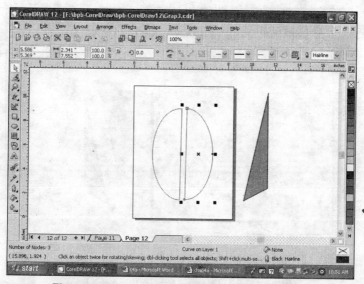

Figure 4.23 The selected ellipse will be deleted.

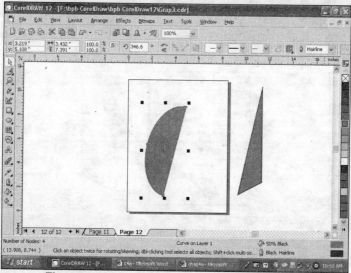

Figure 4.24 The half ellipse rotated and shaded.

Steps to draw the Sun

1. Click the Ellipse tool. Holding the Ctrl key draw a small circle.

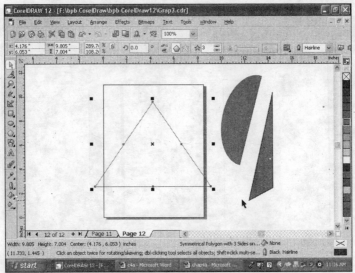

Figure 4.25 Triangle for drawing the boat

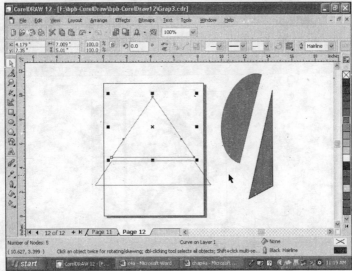

Figure 4.26 The selected triangle will be deleted.

2. Click the Polygon tool. Choose star from the property bar and type number of sides as 20.

3. Drag in the drawing window to draw a small star of 20 sides.

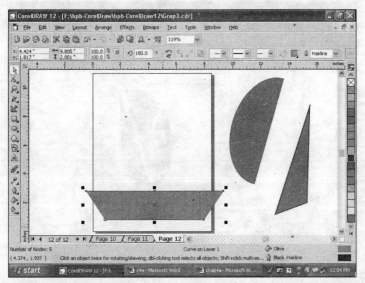

Figure 4.27 The remaining portion of the triangle rotated and shaded.

4. Click the Shape tool and drag any of the nodes inwards to form a star as shown in Figure 4.28.

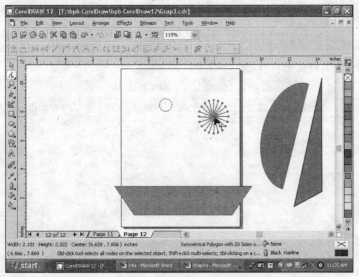

Figure 4.28 A small circle and star of 20 sides drawn to create the sun.

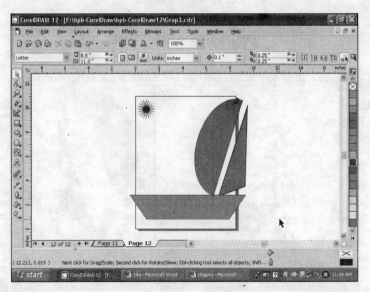

Figure 4.29 Adjust the size and shape of each object to create realistic effect

5. Place the circle at the centre of this star.

6. Select the star and the circle by holding Shift key. If you have any problem in selecting, click on the zoom levels in the standard toolbar and choose 400%.

7. Right click the object and choose Group from the menu that appears.

8. After grouping, zoom out back to 100%.

9. Now choose a dark shade from the color palette.

10. Place these figures at required positions to create drawing as in Figure 4.29.

CHAPTER 5

Working with Text

Creating Artistic Text in Paragraphs

CorelDRAW 12 enables string of text manipulated just as any other graphic objects. Two types of text you can add to drawings. These are:

- Artistic text
- Paragraph text.

Artistic texts are short lines of text to which you can apply a wide range of effects, such as drop shadows etc. Artistic text can be *sized*, *shaped*, *distorted*, *filled*, *outlined* and even converted to *curves*. (See Figure 5.1).

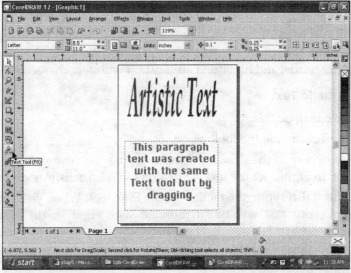

Figure 5.1   The Difference between Artistic and Paragraph Text

Paragraph texts are larger bodies of text that have greater formatting requirements. In fact, paragraph text is more like body text. It can be flowed, indented, hyphenated, put in column, etc. Paragraph text is better suited for editing long blocks of text as seen in Figure 5.1.

When to use Artistic Text?

Use artistic text in the following situations:

- **When you stretch and skew**—Artistic text can easily be scaled and stretched. Paragraph text can also be scaled, stretched or skewed with its frame by using the Alt key.

- **When you mirror, extrude, envelope, or change perspective** —These are the effects that can be applied to artistic text only. The Envelope effect can be applied to paragraph text, but when used with artistic text, envelope and other special effects actually bend characters.

- **For editing character shapes**—If you want to change the very shape of text characters by converting them to curves and then editing the nodes, you must use artistic text.

Note: Convert to curves command, does not work with paragraph text.

Working with Artistic Text

When you create artistic text, you make a graphic image that can be edited like any other graphic in CorelDRAW. You can easily resize or reshape artistic text, edit the graphical aspects, and also the text content and format.

Use artistic text for smaller blocks of text. Icons, Web sites banners, newsletters, master heads, and other text application with few characters.

Creating Artistic Text

To add artistic text, do this:

1. Click the Text tool in the toolbox.
2. Click anywhere in the drawing window using the Text tool and type any sentence. In Figure 5.1 the text written on top is an artistic text.
3. After you finish typing text, click on the Pick tool. When you click on the Pick tool, your text will be surrounded with eight small, square black handles as seen in Figure 5.2. These handles can be dragged to change the size and shape of the Text.

When to use Paragraph Text?

Use Paragraph text in the following situations:

- **To set large blocks of copy**—If artistic text is appropriate for the headline of an article, paragraph text is perfect for the article itself.

  Paragraph text can accommodate thousands of individual paragraphs, and thus, you can create many pages of text.

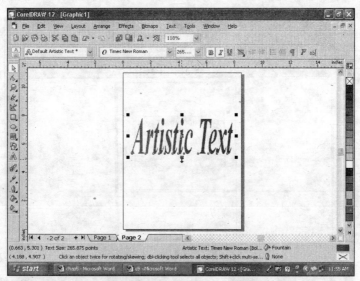

Figure 5.2 Artistic Text with the selection handles

- **To control text flow**—Paragraph text can flow from frame to frame and from page to page. Also, you can easily change the length of the paragraph text.

- **To control the baselines of text**—A handy use for paragraph text is when you want to rotate the whole text along an angle.

Creating Paragraph Text

For creating paragraph text, you must create a text frame for each paragraph text object that you want to add.

To create paragraph text do this:

1. Click the Text tool.
2. Drag the tool in the drawing window to size a paragraph text frame and then type inside the text frame. (See Figure 5.3)

Note: CorelDRAW 12 has a spell checker that flags words not found in the dictionary as you type. It even automatically corrects common spelling or capitalization mistakes.

Switching between Artistic and Paragraph text

If you create text in one form and discover that you really need it to be of other form, you can still convert text from one form to another form easily.

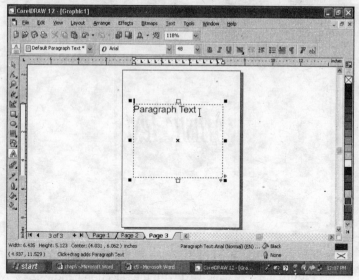

Figure 5.3 Paragraph text frame showing entering text

To switch between artistic and paragraph text, do this:

1. Click the Pick tool and right-click the text.

2. If you want to convert Paragraph text to Artistic text choose Convert To Artistic Text.

3. If you want to convert Artistic text to Paragraph text, choose Convert To Paragraph Text.

To add text on an object do this:

1. Click the Text tool.

2. Move the cursor over the object's outline.

3. Click the object when the cursor changes to the cursor as shown in the top rectangle as in Figure 5.4.

4. Type inside the frame. (See the bottom trapezium in Figure 5.4).

To add text inside an object, do this:

1. Click the Text tool.

2. Move the cursor over the object's outline.

3. Click the object when the cursor changes to the cursor.

4. Type inside the frame. (See Figure 5.5).

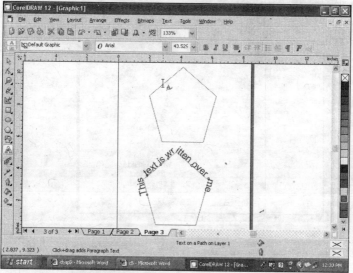

Figure 5.4   Writing text over an object

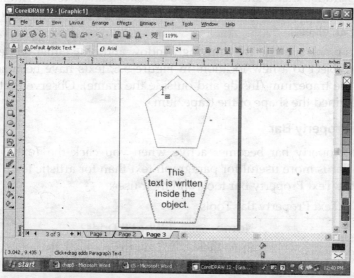

Figure 5.5   Writing a text inside the frame

You can also separate a text frame from a container object. When you do so, the text frame retains the object's shape.

To separate the text frame from an object do this:

1.   Select the object using the Pick tool.

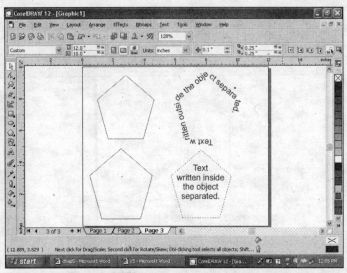

Figure 5.6 Texts separated from the object

2. Click <u>A</u>rrange menu and choose <u>B</u>reak Text Apart (if text written over an object) or choose <u>B</u>reak Paragraph Text inside a Path Apart (if text written inside an object).

3. Click a blank space in the drawing window and drag either the text frame or the object to a new location. In Figure 5.6, texts have been separated from the trapezium (Inside and outside the frame). Observe that the text has retained the shape of the trapezium.

The Text Property Bar

The Text Property bar becomes active when you click the Text Tool. Text Property Bar is more useful for paragraph text than for artistic text. Table 5.1 explains the Text Property Bar tools and their uses.

Table 5.1   Text Property Bar Tools

Tool	Name	What It Does?
Default Artistic Text *	Style List	This drop down list enables you to select style to apply to the selected text.
Arial	Font List	This drop down list enables you to select fonts to apply to the selected text.

(Contd.....)

Tool	Name	What It Does?
12 ⌄	Font Size List	Assigns font sizes to selected text.
B	Bold	Assigns (or turns off) boldface for the selected text.
I	Italic	Assigns (or turns off) italic style for selected text.
U	Underline	Underlines the text in a selected text object.
≣	Horizontal Alignment	Align the block of text i.e. left, right, center, full justify and force full justify.
⇤≣	Decrease Indent	Pulls the text outwards.
⇥≣	Increase Indent	Pushes the text inside.
≔	Show/Hide Bullets	Inserts bullets on the left of text.
A≣	Show/Hide Drop cap	Inserts drop cap at the beginning of a character.
¶	Non-printing Character	Show non-printing characters i.e. tab mark, paragraph mark and blank spaces.
F	Format Text	Opens the Format Text dialog box.
ab[	Edit Text	Opens the Edit Text dialog box.

As you see in Table 5.1, the Text Property Bar enables you to apply all types of formatting to the selected-text objects.

Both the property bar and the **Format Text** dialog box provide full control of *font*, *style* (bold, italic, and so on), and *size*. These controls behave differently in three different selection settings as explained in Table 5.2.

Table 5.2 Effect of formatting text with different selection settings

Selection Setting	Formatting Action
With the entire string of text selected	Format changes affect all of the text.
With text selected within a string or frame	Only the selected text is changed.

(Contd....)

Selection Setting	Formatting Action
With the editing cursor placed in text	Text that you type from that point forward uses the new formatting.

Formatting Text

In CorelDRAW 12, you can set text of size as small as .001 point or as large as 3,000 points. You can apply many formatting styles to selected text, as you do in a word processor. Before you perform any formatting on a text, you must select it.

To select text do this:

1. To select an entire text object, click the object using the Pick tool.
2. To select specific characters, drag across the text using the Text tool.

Format Text Dialog Box

The formatting features of CorelDRAW 12 are categorized into the categories namely, *Character*, *Paragraph*, *Tabs*, *Columns*, and *Effects*. Each of the categories has tab in the Format Text dialog box and are discussed in the following sections. There are five tabs in the Format Text dialog box. You will now learn the features of each one of them as given below.

Character Formatting

To format characters in selected text do this:

1. Select the characters you want to format.
2. Click Text menu and choose Format Text... or press Ctrl+T.
3. Click the Character tab property sheet as in Figure 5.7 appears.
4. Choose a font (typeface) from the Font: list.
5. Set the font Size by choosing a Size from the Size: list.
6. *Alternatively*, after you select the text to which you want to apply formatting, select a new font and font size from the Property bar.
7. Text can also be resized with the Pick tool, by clicking and dragging the corner selection handles. If you want to size paragraph text, you must press Alt key while you drag. Otherwise you size the frame that holds the text, not the text itself. (See Figure 5.8)
8. Choose a style from the Style: list to apply in your text. You can choose between *Normal*, *Normal-Italic*, *Bold* and *Bold-Italics*.

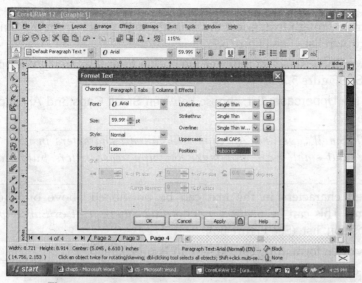

Figure 5.7   Format Text with Character Property tab

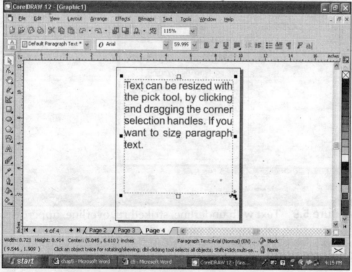

Figure 5.8   Paragraph text to be resized

- To underline text, select the underline option from the Underline: drop down list. (See Figure 5.7)

- To Strikethrough text, select the strikethrough option from the **Strikethru:** drop down list. (See Figure 5.7)

- To Overline text, select the overline option from the **Overline:** drop down list. (See Figure 5.7)

9. From the **Uppercase:** list, choose between **Small Caps** and **All Caps**. (See Figure 5.7)

Note: Both Small caps and All caps will convert characters in your text to uppercase. But small caps will make the uppercase letters but smaller in height.

10. Selected characters in the text can be positioned above or below the baseline. This can be printed by choosing *Superscript* or *Subscript* from the **Position:** list. (See Figure 5.7)

Above written formatting can be seen in Figure 5.9.

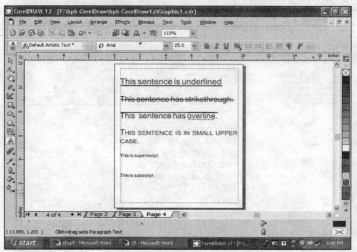

Figure 5.9   Text with underline, strikethru, overline, uppercase, subscript and superscript applied

Paragraph Formatting

The Paragraph tab provides options for formatting the Paragraph.

To format paragraphs do this:

1. Select the Paragraph text.
2. Click **Text** menu and choose **Format Text...** . Or **Ctrl+T**.
3. Click the **Paragraph** tab property sheet appears as in Figure 5.10.

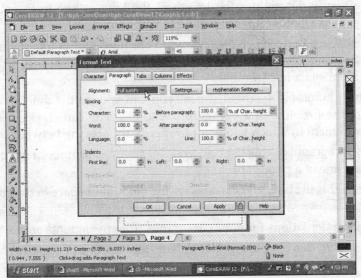

Figure 5.10 Paragraph tab property sheet in the Format Text

4. Choose alignment from the **Alignment**: list box, to apply in your text. For example, *None*, *Left*, *Center*, *Right*, *Full Justify* or *Force Justify* from the Alignment list. Different types of alignment applied to text and shown in Figure 5.11.

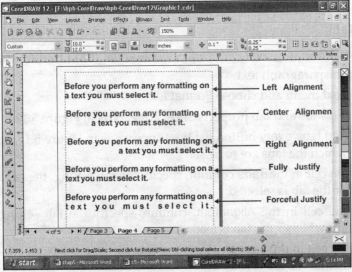

Figure 5.11 Different types of alignment

5. Force justify determines the length of the longest line in the paragraph and adjusts all other lines to extend to that point.

6. Adjust space between characters, words or lines within a paragraph from the Spacing area. You can also indicate spacing above and below paragraphs in a text frame.

    Before paragraph: In this list box, you can specify the amount of space before the first line of a paragraph. And also you can choose the unit of measurement in which you want to specify the spacing between the lines.

    After paragraph: In this list box, you can specify the amount of space after the last line of a paragraph.

    Line: In this list box, you can specify the amount of space between the text lines.

7. Specify indentations for your paragraphs from the Indents area.

    First line: In this list box, specify indents the first line of paragraph text.

    Left: In this list box, specify a hanging indent in which all but the first line of text is indented.

    Right: In this list box, specify indents for the right side of paragraph text.

8. In the Text Direction area, choose the orientation from the Orientation: drop down list. You can choose vertical or horizontal orientation as per your need.

9. Click Apply and then Click OK.

Setting Tabs

Tab is used for setting the tab distance, tab alignment and trailing character.

1. Select the paragraph text.

2. Click Text menu and choose Format text... .

3. Click the Tabs and tab property sheet appears as in Figure 5.12.

4. Click Add tabs every button list box, appears as in Figure 5.13, specify the tab at which the tabs are to be set.

5. Click the cell in the Tabs column, specify the tab setting, the tab type, and whether the tab is selected.

6. Click the cell in the Alignment: column, specify the tab setting, the tab type, and whether the tab is lead.

7. Click the cell in the Leader... column, specify the tab setting, the tab type, and whether the tab is selected.

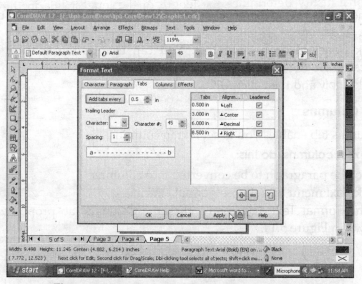

Figure 5.12 Tabs in the Format Text dialog box

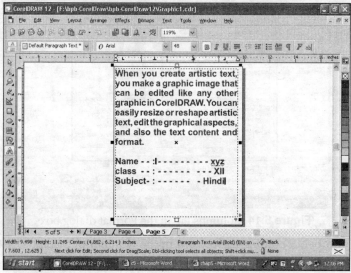

Figure 5.13 Different tab settings with Trailing Characters

8. The + (plus) button indicates add a tab, and (–) button indicates delete a selected tab. And the third button (×) indicates delete all tabs.

9. In the Trailing Leader area, choose the Character: list, specify the character for a leader tab.

10. Click Spacing: drop down list. You can change the spacing between characters in the trailing leader tab.

11. Click Apply and then click OK.

Setting Columns

The columns tab enables you to set text in columns.

To set text in columns, do this:

1. Select the paragraph to be converted into columns.

2. Click Text menu and choose Format text... .

3. In the Format Text dialog box, click the Columns tab property sheet as shown in Figure 5.14.

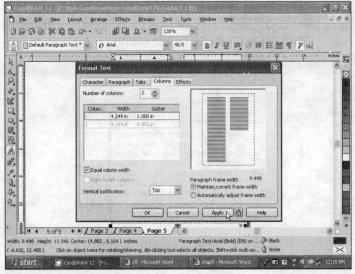

Figure 5.14 Columns tab in the Format dialog box

4. Type number of columns you want in the Number of columns: list box.

5. Specify column width and gutter. Gutter represents the spacing between each column.

6. If you want columns to be of equal width, click the Equal column width: check box.

7. In the Vertical justification: drop down list, specify the vertical justification you want for columns

8. Click Apply and then click OK.

Using Effects

The Effects tab is useful for inserting drop cap, bullets etc.

To use effects tab, do this:

1. Select the paragraph to which you want to apply special effects.
2. Click Text menu and choose Format text... .
3. In the Format Text dialog box, click the Effects tab property sheet appears as in Figure 5.15.

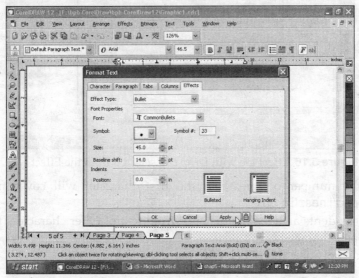

Figure 5.15 Effect tab with Bullet selected from the Effect type.

4. Choose Bullet from the Effect Type: drop down list. (See Figure 5.15)

    In the Font properties area:

    Font: drop down list, choose a font for the bullet.

    Symbol: drop down list, and select desired symbol font.

    Symbol #: specify the number of the symbol you want to use as a bullet.

    Size: list box, specify the size of the bullet.

    Baseline shift: specify the distance by which the bullet is offset from the baseline.

5. In the Indents area choose the position where you want the bullets to appear.

6. In the **Effect Type**: Choose Drop cap, if you want the first character in your paragraph to be of large size than the rest of the characters. (See Figure 5.16)

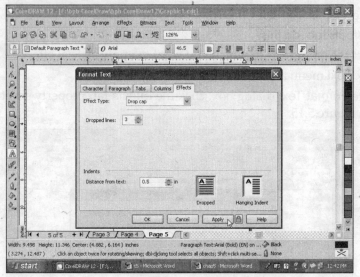

Figure 5.16 Effect tab with Drop cap selected from the Effect type.

7. Set the number of lines that the first character will cover from the **Dropped lines**: list box.

8. In the Indents area set the distance from text of other characters from the dropped character.

9. Click Apply and then Click OK.

Using Edit Text Feature

The Edit Text dialog box is very helpful, when you are editing large amount of text.

To use edit text do this:

1. Select text object.

2. Click **Text** menu and choose the **Edit Text**... The **Edit Text** dialog box appears as in Figure 5.17.

3. The **Edit Text** dialog box is a mini word processor in Windows. You can insert or delete text here. The **Edit Text** dialog box will even underline words not found in the dictionary with red line. You can instantly look up correct spellings by right-clicking a word, as shown in Figure 5.17.

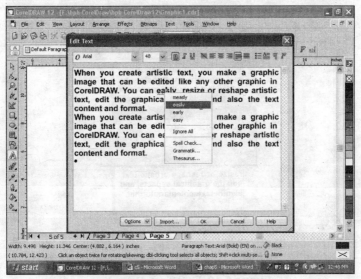

Figure 5.17 Edit Text dialog box

4. To add formatting, click on the Font attributes in the toolbar of Edit dialog box. Attributes assigned in this way will apply to the text.

5. When you have edited and assigned formatting to any text, click OK in the Edit Text dialog box.

6. The results will be visible in the CorelDRAW window.

Note: The Edit Text dialog box is not fully WYSIWYG (What You See Is What You Get). You have to click OK and view the results in the CorelDRAW window to see the exact effect of font attributes assigned to selected text.

When you rotate text, you can edit or reformat it. You might find it easier to edit rotated text in the Edit Text dialog box.

Using Find and Replace

You can search text automatically using find and replace text facility in CorelDRAW.

To search for a word in a block of text, do this:

1. Select the block of text.

2. Click Edit menu highlight Find and Replace and choose Find Text... . The Find Text dialog box appears as in Figure 5.18.

3. Type the text you want to find in the Find what: box.

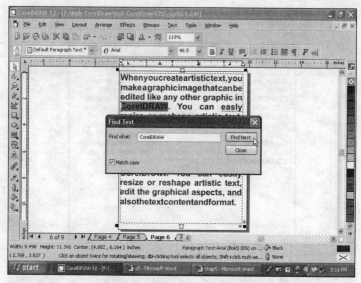

Figure 5.18 Find Text dialog box

4. Click **Find Next** button to begin the search again. After searching is completed, click **Close** button.

5. If you want to find the exact case of the text you specified, enable the **Match case** check box.

Change Case

CorelDRAW provides facilities to capitalize any text by using the Change Case command.

To apply the Change Case command do this:

1. Select the text, for which you want to change capitalization.

2. Click **Text** menu and choose **Change Case...** or Press **Shift+F3** keys together. The dialog appears as in Figure 5.19.

The Options in Change Case dialog box, are discussed below:

Sentence—The first character of the first word is capitalized.

Lowercase—All the characters are in lowercase.

Uppercase—All characters are in uppercase.

Title case—The first letter of each word is capitalized.

Toggle case—All uppercase letters become lowercase and all lowercase letters become uppercase.

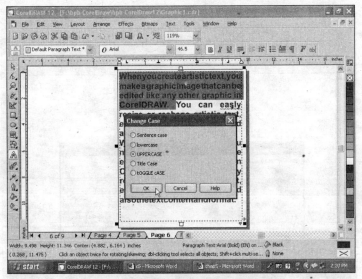

Figure 5.19 Change Case dialog box

Using Spell Check

Spell check lets you check the text in several ways. You can use Spell check to check all of the spelling in a drawing, a portion of a drawing, or only selected text.

To Spell Check selected text do this:

1. Select the text you want to check.
2. Click the Text menu, highlight Writing tools and choose Spell check... .
3. The Writing Tools dialog box appears as in Figure 5.20. Click the Spell Checker tab. (This is selected by default).
4. In the Replace with: text box, choose the text that you want to replace the misspelled text.
5. In the Replacements: CorelDRAW displays the various options for the misspelled words text box, select a word and click the Replace button.
6. Click the Skip Once or Skip All button, to ignore the wrong word(s).
7. Click the Undo button to undo the spelling change.
8. After making changes, click Close button.

Grammar checking text

Grammatik lets you check the text in this way. You can check the grammar in the selected text only.

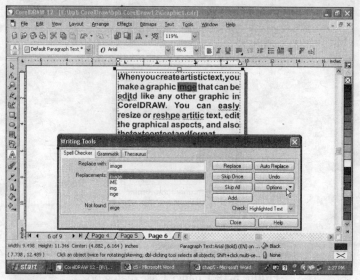

Figure 5.20 Writing Tools dialog box with Spell checker tab

To check Grammar do this:

1. Select the sentence or paragraph for which the grammar needs to be checked.

2. Click the **T**ext menu and choose **W**riting **Tools**. In the **Writing Tools** dialog box, click **Grammatik** tab property sheet as in Figure 5.21 appears.

3. In the **Rep**lacements: text box, select the word or sentences, click the **Replace** button.

4. In the **New sentence:** list box, it displays a new sentence using the selected word in the **Replacements:** list box.

5. The mistaken words are highlighted in the **Spelling:** list box.

6. Click the **Skip O**nce or **Skip A**ll button, to ignore the grammar mistake.

7. Click the **U**n**do** button to undo the spelling change.

8. After making changes, click the **C**lose button.

Using Thesaurus

The Thesaurus lets you look up options such as Synonyms, Antonyms, and Related words, depending on the language and version of Thesaurus you are using.

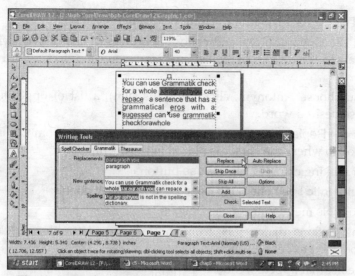

Figure 5.21 Grammatik tab in the Writing Tools dialog box

To use Thesaurus, do this:

1. Select a word within a string or frame
2. Click **Text** menu highlight **Writing Tools** and choose **Thesaurus...** . See Figure 5.22.

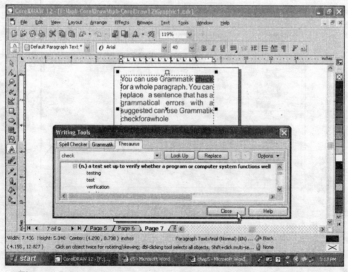

Figure 5.22 Thesaurus tab in the Writing Tools dialog box

3. The Thesaurus, display the selected word in the list box.

4. Click the **Option** button and choose Synonym. A list of synonym words appears in the bottom of the list box. Now you can select a word from the list.

   If you choose Antonym, click the (plus sign), a list of opposite appear, choose desired word.

5. Click the **Replace** button, to replace and insert words from the Thesaurus list box to where the cursor is placed in the document.

6. After making changes, click **Close** button.

To get automatic spell checking done by CorelDRAW do this:

1. Click **Tools** menu and choose **Options**... .

2. In the **Options** dialog box, from the menu on left side, click on the + symbol next to Text.

3. In the list that appears, choose spelling.

4. Check the perform Automatic Spell Checking check box. (See Figure 5.23)

5. Spell check will be done automatically, as you type the text.

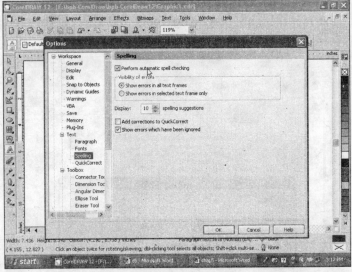

Figure 5.23 Spelling options in the Options dialog box

CHAPTER 6

Advanced Text Work

Fitting Text to Path

You can position artistic text along the path of an open object (for example, a line) or a closed object (for example, a square).

After you fit text to a path, you can adjust the text's position relative to that path. For example, you can place the text on the opposite side of the path, or you can adjust the distance between the text and the path.

To fit text to a path, do this:

1. Draw a Curve using the Freehand tool.
2. Click Text menu and choose Fit Text to path.
3. Type along the path. You can fit text to any object. (See Figure 6.1)

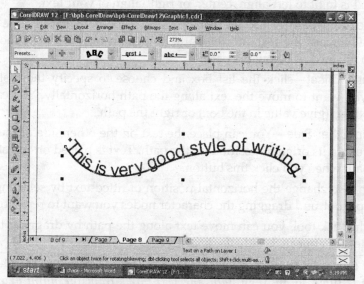

Figure 6.1   Fitting text to path

On the Text on Curve/Object property bar as in Figure 6.2, choose from the following options:

Plus button – Add preset to the presets list box.

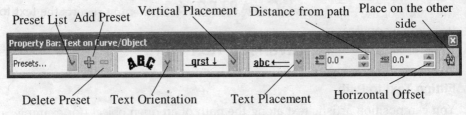

Figure 6.2 Text on Curve/Object property bar

(Minus) button – Delete Preset from the presets list box.

Text Orientation—click the drop down list and choose the text typeface and size oriented on the path.

Vertical Placement—click the drop down list and choose the vertical position of the text on the path, for example you want place the text above, below the path.

Text Placement—click the drop down list and choose the horizontal position if the text is to fit to left-align, center, or right-align of your text.

Distance from path—click the list box and choose to specify the vertical distance between the text and the path. You can move your text above (give value in the box) or below the path.

Horizontal Offset—click the list box and choose to specify the distance by which you want to move the text along the path horizontally. You can move your text left (give value in the box) or right the path.

Place on Other Side—You can place the text on the other side of the path or return text to its original position on the path. Text is placed on the other side of the path when you click this button.

You can also change the horizontal position of fitted text by selecting it with the Shape tool, and dragging the character nodes you want to reposition.

Using the Pick tool, you can move text along the path by dragging the small red node that appears beside the text.

Note: If the text is fitted to a closed path, the text is centered along the path. If the text is fitted to an open path, the text flows from the point of insertion. You cannot fit text to the path of another text object. You can also fit text to a path by clicking the Text tool, pointing over an object, clicking where you want the text to begin, and typing the text.

CorelDRAW treats text fitted to a path as one object. However, you can separate the text from the object if you no longer want it to be part of the path. When you separate text from a curved or closed path, the text retains the shape of the object to which it was fitted. Straightening reverts the text to its original appearance.

To separate text from a path do this:

1. Select the fitted text using the Pick tool.
2. Click Arrange menu and choose Break Apart (See Figure 6.3)

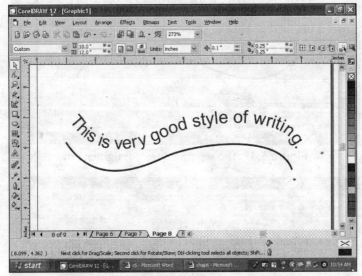

Figure 6.3 The text separated from the path

To straighten text do this:

1. Select the fitted text using the Pick tool.
2. Separate the text from the path.
3. Click Text menu and choose Straighten text. (See Figure 6.4)

Flowing Text around an Object

You can flow the text around an object in CorelDRAW. The text will appear to have adapted its shape according to the object. This is done using the Interactive tool flyout (See in Figure 6.5). This figure shows how the image appears to have been wrapped by the paragraph text.

To flow text around an object, do this:

1. Click the Text tool.
2. Create a text frame, in the drawing window.

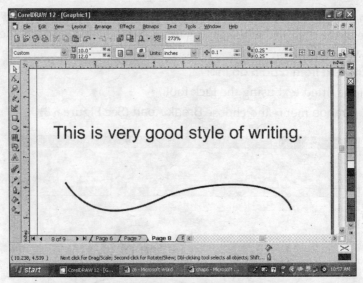

Figure 6.4   The separated text straighten out

Figure 6.5   Text flow around the object

3. Type or copy some paragraph text.

4. Import a clipart in the drawing window. Select the text and click the Interactive Envelope tool in the tool box. You can see in the text frame a small handle. Call it as node.

5. Click the node and drag it up over the object. As soon as you do so, the text will instantly wrap around this new shape. (See Figure 6.5)

Flowing Text within an Object

You can flow the text within an object that is, the text flows within an object taking the shape of the object.

To flow text within an object, do this:

1. Click the pick tool.
2. Import any picture, in the drawing window.
3. Create a text frame, type some text inside the frame.
4. Select the text with the pick tool.
5. Drag the text while holding the right mouse button and place it inside the picture.
6. Release the mouse button. The options appear as in Figure 6.6. Click the Powerclip Inside the object. (See Figure 6.7).

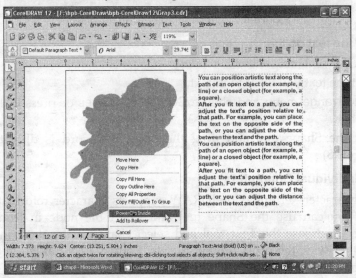

Figure 6.6 Right click the mouse the options appears

7. You can also place text inside basic shapes like rectangle, circle, polygon etc.

Untext

What do we mean by untext? It is the text that is no longer treated as text by CorelDRAW.

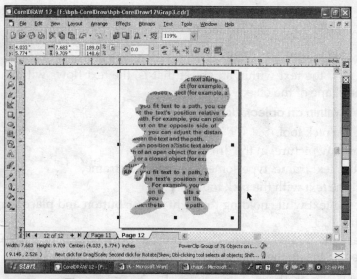

Figure 6.7 Flowing text inside the object

To untext the text do this:

1. Click the Text tool.
2. Select the text you want to untext.
3. Click <u>A</u>rrange menu and choose Con<u>v</u>ert to Curves or press Ctrl+Q keys together.
4. Click the Shape tool and drag the node, the word is distorted. (See Figure 6.8)

Editing Individual Characters

Besides character kerning, CorelDRAW supports character reformatting. To do this, you can use the Shape tool and select the node in front of the character, or choose the Text tool and select characters by dragging across them. Either way, the property bar and the Format Text dialog are the used for reformatting characters.

To edit individual character do this:

1. Click the Text tool.
2. Create a Paragraph text and Artistic text.
3. Now change the size and color of character 'A' of the artistic text and the character `P' of the paragraph text. (See Figure 6.9)
4. First select the node of 'A' with shape tool. Then click on a color from the color palette and choose a larger size from the Property bar.

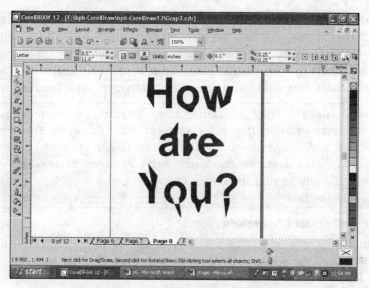

Figure 6.8 The word Hello is distorted

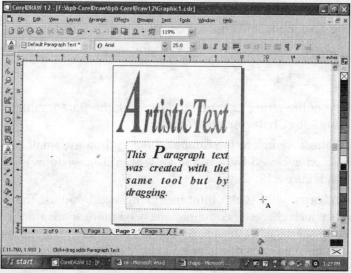

Figure 6.9 Kerning Individual Character with the shape tool

5. Now using Text tool select 'P' of paragraph text, and change its color and font size as explained above. Figure 6.9 shows the result of the above process.

The Text tool is more intuitive, providing a standard text cursor for selecting text, but the Shape tool has the advantage of allowing you to select non-contiguous characters. Select one character, hold Shift key and then select others anywhere in the string. You can also use the Shape tool to rotate individual characters with the Angle of Rotation control on the Property bar.

Note: Individual character formatting is overwritten by changes made to a text string's size or style. If you format characters using the Shape tool and then format the entire string in the conventional manner, your custom formatting will be lost for those attributes changes in the entire string. Therefore, globally format the entire string first, and then locally format the individual characters.

Kerning Individual Characters

Individual adjustment of characters is called kerning. To kern characters means to adjust the space between the characters. Capital letters often need manual kerning to look better.

To kern character do this:

1. Select the characters you want to kern.
2. Click the Text menu and choose Format Text... or Ctrl+T.
3. In the Format Text dialog box click Character tab to set a value for Range kerning.
4. Click OK.
5. Select the entire string or frame to text, click the Paragraph tab and then enter values for Character and Word.
6. Select the text, switch to the Shape tool, and drag the small thingamabob (i.e. the area enclosed by a rectangle with a drop shadow) in or out, as shown in Figure 6.10.

CorelDRAW carry with it the built-in intelligence to adjust the kerning. It understands which character combinations need more space among them and which need less. This is referred to as kerning pairs. Invariably, however, text at large sizes or in all caps needs to be scrutinized for proper kerning. Figure 6.11 shows various types of kerning.

Working with Text Styles

A text style is a set of text settings such as font type and size. Text style also include fill and outline attributes. There are two types of text styles: artistic and paragraph as discussed in the previous chapter. You can also change the properties of default artistic and paragraph text. For example, you can change the properties of default artistic text, so that every artistic text object you create has the same formatting.

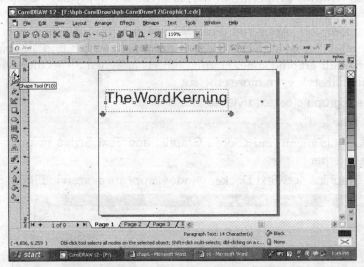

Figure 6.10 Kerning text with the shape tool

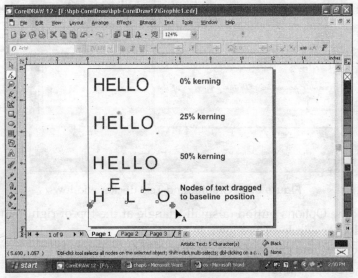

Figure 6.11 Different types of kerning

You can as well create a graphic or text style from scratch or from the properties of an existing object, at which time the style is saved. When you apply a style to an object, CorelDRAW overrides the existing text or graphic properties with the properties of the style you are applying. To use the style in another drawing, you can copy the style to the new drawing or save the style in a template. After you create a style, you can edit its properties and find any object using a given style. For example, you can find all objects that use the default graphic style. Finding objects assigned a specific style makes editing in that style even more efficient.

To create a graphic or text style do this:

1. Select the text.

2. Click T**o**ols menu and choose **Graphic and Text St**y**les** or press **Ctrl+F5** keys together.

3. The **Graphics and Text** Docker window appears as seen in Figure 6.12

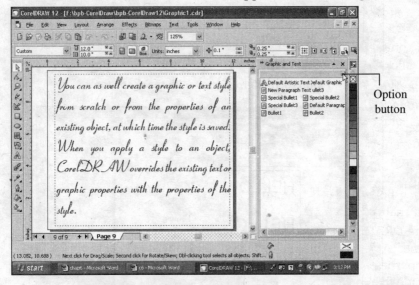

Figure 6.12 Graphic and Text docker window

4. Click the **Options** button (a small triangle at the top of right-hand side of the docker window) as shown in Figure 6.12.

5. Click **New**, and choose **Paragraph Text Style**.

6. In the **Graphic and Text** docker window, select New Paragraph text, and right click button and choose **Properties… .**

7. The **Options** dialog box appears as in Figure 6.13.

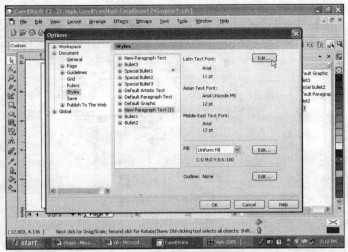

Figure 6.13 Style options in the Options dialog box

8. Click **Edit**... button to apply changes in the **Format Text** dialog box.
9. You can apply fill, or outline in the selected text.
10. Click **OK**.

Note: When you create a style from an existing object, CorelDRAW does not automatically apply the style to the object. If you want the object to use the style, you must apply the style.

You can create a graphic or text style from any selected object by right-clicking the object, in the shortcut menu that appears as in Figure 6.14 highlight **Styles** and choose **Save Style Properties**.... The **Save Style As** dialog box appears as shown in Figure 6.15. Type a name in the **Name:** box, and enable the **Fill** and/or **Outline** check boxes.

CorelDRAW renames or delete the style by adding a number to the style name. At any point, you can rename a style. You can also change the properties of an object back to its previous style if you made a mistake or decide that the previous style was better suited to that object.

To delete a style do this:

1. Select the style you want to delete.
2. Right click and **Delete**.

To rename a style do this:

1. Select the style you want to rename.
2. Right click and choose **Rename**.

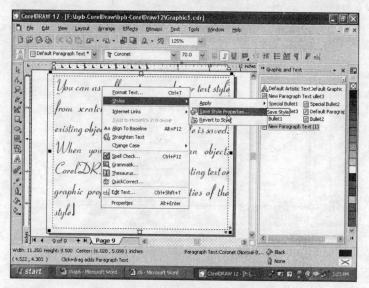

Figure 6.14 Save Style Properties

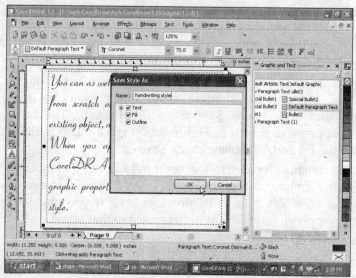

Figure 6.15 Save Style As dialog box

Linking Frames

Linking frames enables or directs the flow of text from one text frame to another to incase the amount of text that exceeds the size of the first text frame. However, shrinking or enlarging a linked paragraph text frame or changing the size of the text automatically adjusts the amount of text in the next text frame. You can also create and link paragraph text frames before you begin typing text in the first text frame.

You can link a paragraph text frame to an open or closed object. When you link a paragraph text frame to an open object (for example, a line), the text flows along the path of the line. Linking a text frame to a closed object (for example, a rectangle) inserts a paragraph text frame and directs the flow of text inside the object. If text exceeds the open or closed path, you can link it to another text frame or object. You can also link to paragraph text frames and objects across pages.

After linking paragraph text frames, you can redirect the flow from one object or text frame to another. When you select the text frame or object, a blue arrow indicates the direction of the text flow. You can also hide or display the arrows that indicate the direction of the text flow.

If all the text does not fit in a single frame, then you can flow it from one frame to another. This technique is essential for laying out presentation and documents that arrange text in multiple frames.

To resize the text do this:

1. Create a Paragraph text frame.
2. You can resize text to fit a frame by selecting the text frame.
3. Click the Text menu and choose Fit Text to Frame. (See Figure 6.16)

To Flow Text from one frame into another do this:

1. Select a text frame using the Pick tool.

   Drag up on the bottom handle (not the shape-sizing handle). Keep making your text frame smaller until, not all the text you typed fits into the frame. When text does not fit in the frame, the bottom sizing handle changes from an open square to one with a triangle in it. (See Figure 6.17)

2. Use the Text tool in the toolbox to draw a new text frame.
3. Select the original text frame with the pick tool, (the frame with overflow text) and click on the triangle at the bottom of the frame to "load" the cursor with the text that did not fit in the frame.
4. Point to the new text frame into which you will continue the text. A large black arrow appears, as shown in Figure 6.17.
5. Click to pour the overflow text into the new frame. After you continue text, the bottom handle of the first frame displays a box with lines,

meaning this text is continued. A line appears connecting the original frame to the "continued to" frame, as seen in Figure 6.18.

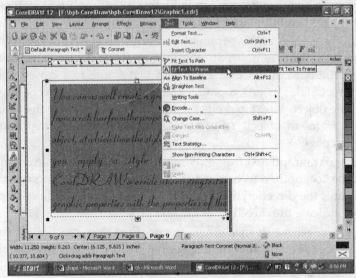

Figure 6.16 Selecting text Fit text to frame

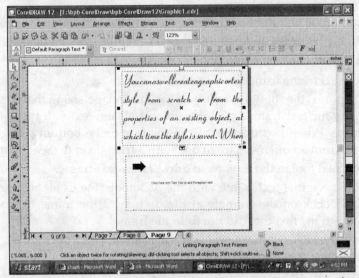

Figure 6.17 A black a.row indicating text flow into the new text frame

6. Enlarge your second text frame until all the continued text fits. When there is no more text to display, the bottom handle of the final frame is displayed as an open square as seen in Figure 6.18.

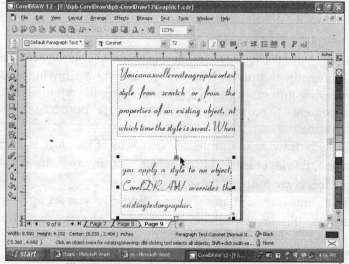

Figure 6.18 Enlarging second text frame

7. The above steps can be repeated for flowing text frame to other objects as seen in Figure 6.19.

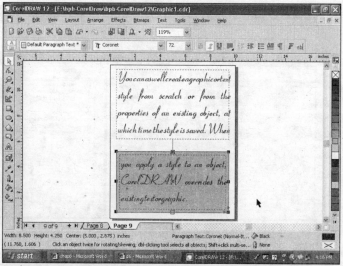

Figure 6.19 The text flowing to an object

CHAPTER 7

Working with Layers and Symbols

Working with Layers

CorelDRAW 12 allows you to arrange elements in complex drawings using Layering. Layering technique helps in organizing a drawing and you can divide a drawing into multiple layers. Each layer will contain a portion of the drawing's contents. You can apply changes to a portion of the drawing without affecting the rest.

By default, each drawing in CorelDRAW consists of four layers. These are:

- Layer 1, this layer is the one on which your figure is drawn.
- Grid, this layer contains the grid that you set up.
- Guides, this layer contains the guidelines that you set up.
- Desktop, this layer contains drawings or objects which can be used repeatedly. This is so because this layer can be accessed regardless of which layer or page you are working on.

To create layers do this:

1. Click **Tools** menu and choose **Object Manager**. The Object Manager Docker window appears as shown in Figure 7.1.

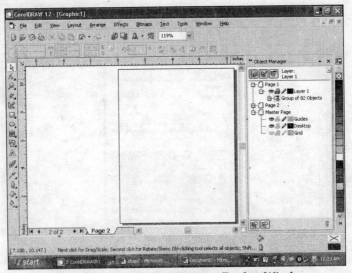

Figure 7.1 The Object Manager Docker Window

2. To create a new layer, click the small triangle at the top-right corner of the window. *Alternatively*, you can right click on any open space in the Docker window.

3. From the menu that opens up, choose New Layer (See Figure 7.2).

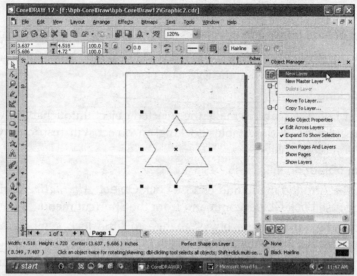

Figure 7.2 Adding new layer from the Object Manager Docker window

A layer has three basic properties that you can control. These properties can be controlled through the docker window only. You can see in the docker window that each layer is accompanied by three icons namely eyes, print and pencil. These icons can be used to control the layer properties.

Icon	Layer Property	Description
	Visibility	Click the eye to make a layer visible or invisible
	Printability	Click the printer icon on the docker window to make a layer printable or unprintable
	Editability	Click the pencil icon to lock or unlock a layer. Locking a layer means that no activity can take place on it at all

To move an object between layers, do this:

1. Select the object and click the small triangle at the top right corner of the window.

2. From the menu that appears, choose Move To Layer....

3. Click the layer to which you want to move the object.

To delete a layer do this:

1. In the docker window, right click the layer which you want to delete.

2. From the menu that appears choose Delete.

To display or hide a layer do this:

1. In the docker window, Click the Eye icon beside the layer name.

2. The layer is hidden when the Eye icon is grayed.

Object Locking

The Object Locking features make the selected object untouchable, even if the layer it resides on it is editable. Locking an object will restrict any further modification on the object.

To lock an object do this:

1. Click the Arrange menu and choose Lock Object. *Alternatively*, right click and choose Lock Object command from the Shortcut menu.

2. The handles around the object change to little lock symbols as shown around the star in Figure 7.3.

Now, you cannot *move, resize, rotate, recolor* or *delete* the rectangle. The object remains as it is till you unlock it.

To unlock an object do this:

1. Select the object you want to unlock.

2. Click Arrange menu and choose Unlock.

Now you can modify, copy or delete these objects as needed.

Working with Symbols

CorelDRAW 12, you create objects and save them as symbols. Symbols are defined once and can be referenced many times in a drawing. Each time you insert a symbol into a drawing, you create an instance of the symbol. Symbol definitions, as well as information about instances, are stored in a symbol manager, which is part of the CorelDRAW (CDR) file. Using symbols for objects that appear many times in a drawing helps to reduce the file size.

Symbols are created from objects. When you convert an object to a symbol, the new symbol is added to the **Symbol manager**, and the selected object becomes an instance. Any changes you make will affect all instances in a drawing. The selection handles for symbols differ from those for objects. Selection handles for symbols are blue; selection handles for objects are black.

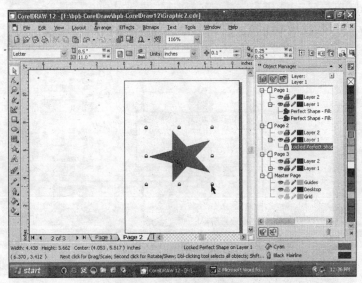

Figure 7.3 Locked Object

To convert an object to a symbol do this:

1. Select an object or multiple objects.
2. Click Edit menu, choose Symbol, and select New Symbol.
3. Create New Symbol dialog box appears as shown in Figure 7.4. Here, you have to give the name of the symbol.
4. Click OK

Note: Symbols cannot span layers. If you convert objects on different layers to a symbol, the objects are combined on the topmost object's layer as seen in the docker window of Figure 7.4.

To rename a symbol do this:

1. Click Edit menu, choose Symbol, and select Symbol manager. Symbol Manager docker window appears as shown in Figure 7.5.
2. If you want to name or rename the symbol, double-click the symbol's name box, and type a name. (See Figure 7.5)

To insert a symbol instance do this:

1. In the Symbol manager docker window, select the symbol from the symbol list.
2. If you want the symbol scaled automatically to match the current drawing scale, enable the Scale to world units button.

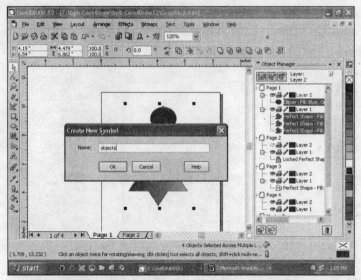

Figure 7.4 Convert an object to symbol

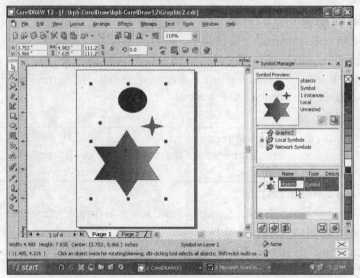

Figure 7.5 Renaming the symbol in the docker window

3. Click the Insert symbol button. (See Figure 7.6)

To edit a symbol do this:

1. Select the symbol on the drawing window. (See Figure 7.6)

2. Click Edit Symbol button on the bottom of the docker window.

3. Modify the objects on the drawing page. (See Figure 7.6)

4. After that click on the **Finish editing object** tab in the bottom left corner of the drawing window.

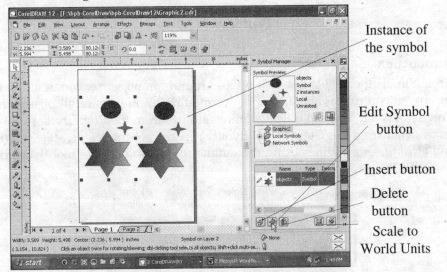

Instance of the symbol

Edit Symbol button

Insert button

Delete button

Scale to World Units

Figure 7.6 Editing a symbol in the drawing window.

5. Changes made to a symbol are automatically made to all instances in the active drawing. (See Figure 7.7)

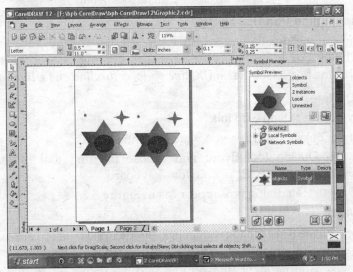

Figure 7.7 Changes applied in the instance of the symbol

CHAPTER 8

Outline Tool

Introduction

An outline is the visible line that wraps around an object i.e. comes around an object. You can assign and apply formatting to outlines of all objects in CorelDRAW 12. You can quickly define outlines from the Property Bar or in more detail from the Outline Tool flyout. You can set the *width, style, color* and *attributes* of outlines using the outline flyout. The outline tool flyout is shown in Figure 8.1.

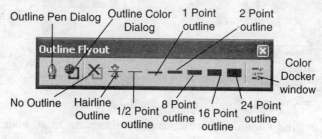

Figure 8.1   The Outline tool flyout ·

Using the Outline Pen Dialog Box

To set the outline details you will need to use the Outline Pen dialog box. Outline dialog box offers many features for outlining objects. You can also use the Outline box to set the *width, line style, color, line ends, line caps,* etc.

Setting Outline

To specify outline settings, do this:

1. Select the object for which you want to define settings.
2. Click the Outline tool flyout and choose the first tool in the flyout. *Alternatively*, press F12, key on your keyboard.
3. The Outline Pen dialog box appears as in Figure 8.2.

Outline Width

1. In the Outline Pen dialog box, click on the Width drop down list and choose a width and unit of measurement for drawing the outline.
2. Click Ok. *Alternatively*, the outline width can be set from the preset buttons in the Outline tool flyout.

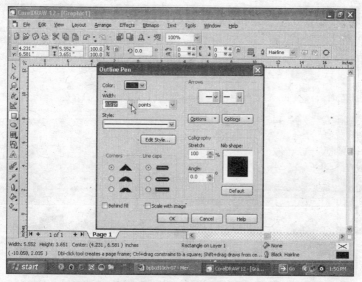

Figure 8.2 The Outline Pen dialog box

To set Outline width from the preset buttons, do this:

1. Select the object using Pick tool, the width of outline of which you want to change.

2. Click on the Outline tool in the toolbox.

3. Choose from one of the Preset buttons. You can choose thickness range from hairline width to 16 point thickness. (See Figure 8.3)

4. The thickness will be applied to the outline of the selected object.

Outline Styles

To set outline styles do this:

1. In the Outline Pen dialog box, choose a line from the Style drop down list. (See Figure 8.4)

2. You can choose *Solid*, *Dash* like or *dot* like line styles from this list (See Figure 8.4). You can also create line styles of your choice.

To create your own line style do this:

1. In the Outline Pen dialog box, choose a style other than solid line, from the Style: drop down list.

2. Click on the Edit Style... button. Edit Line Style dialog box appears as in Figure 8.5.

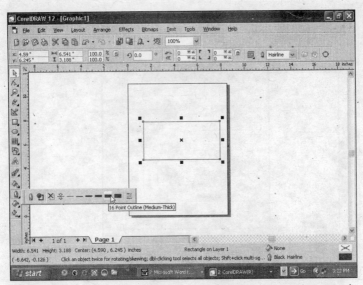

Figure 8.3 Choosing Outline width from the preset button of Outline tool flyout

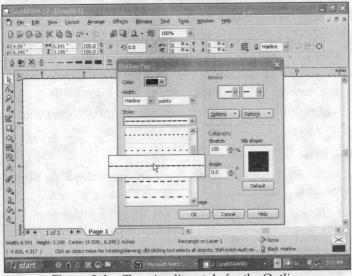

Figure 8.4 Choosing line style for the Outline

3. In the Edit Line Style dialog box, move the vertical bar to the right or to the left for turning the dots on the line *ON* or *OFF*. Depending on the

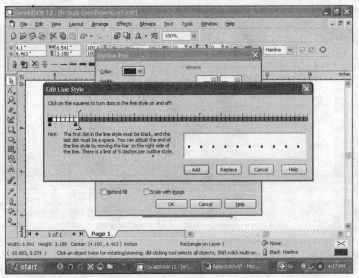

Figure 8.5 Editing line style to create a new line style

distance, the bar moves to right or left, the number of dots that are turned *on* or *off* increase.

4. Click Add.

5. Click OK in the Outline Pen dialog box.

Outline Color

To set color to the outline, do this:

1. In the Outline Pen dialog box, choose a color for the outline from the Color: drop down box. (See Figure 8.6)

2. If the color of your choice is not available in the current palette, click Other....

3. A Select Color dialog box appears as in Figure 8.7. Here you can change the *palettes, choose spot colors* and also you can mix your own CMYK, RGB or HSB colors.

4. Click OK.

Outline Corners

To set Outline corners, do this:

1. Select the object for which you want to set outline corners.

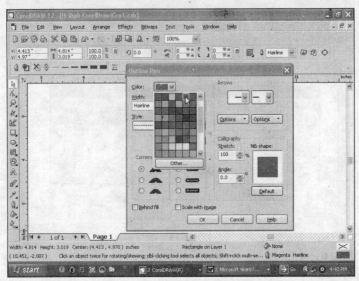

Figure 8.6   Selecting color for the outline from the Color drop down list

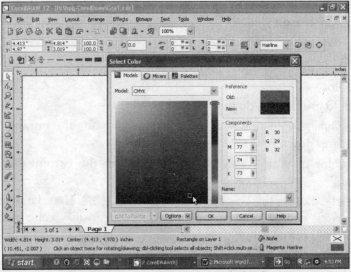

Figure 8.7   The Select Color dialog box.

2. Click the Outline tool flyout and choose Outline Pen Dialog tool.

3. In the Outline Pen dialog box, from the Corners area choose a corner type for your outline.

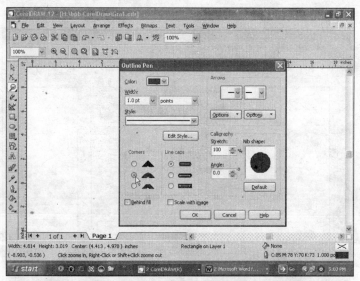

Figure 8.8 Select the corner type of your choice

4. Click on the radio button of the chosen corner (See Figure 8.8)

- The corner type shown at the top creates sharp corners.

- The middle one creates rounded corners.

- The bottom one creates corners that are blunt or cut at the meeting point

5. Click **OK**.

Setting Outline Arrows

CorelDRAW lets you define outlines in the form of arrows to your objects. A wide variety of arrows are available and you can choose an arrow style of your choice from the exhaustive range available.

To set and edit arrow at the line ends, do this:

1. Select a line or curve.

2. In the **Outline Pen** dialog box, from the **Arrow** area, choose an arrow type of your choice from the two arrow boxes.

3. The arrow box at the left specifies the arrow that will appear at the starting point of the line. The arrow box at the right specifies the arrow for the ending point of your line.

4. If you want to modify the width or length of the arrow head, Click on **Options** drop down list and choose **New**.... The **Edit Arrowhead** box appears as in Figure 8.9.

5. In the **Arrowhead Editor** dialog box, resize or reshape your arrowhead and reposition it in relation to the line.

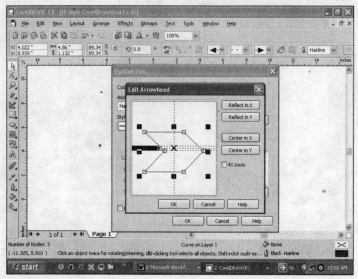

Figure 8.9 Modifying the arrowhead in the Edit Arrowhead dialog box.

6. It is a possibility that while resizing your arrowhead; it goes off the centre of the line. Click the **Centre in X** or **Centre in Y** button to place your arrow precisely at the centre of the line.

7. Click on the **Reflect in X** button to flip the arrowhead horizontally.

8. Click on the **Reflect in Y** button to flip it vertically.

9. Click **OK** after you finish working on selected arrow.

Applying Calligraphic Outlines

Calligraphic lines are similar to the lines drawn using a calligraphic pen. Such lines change their thickness according to the direction of the line. Line's thickness also varies depending upon the angle of the pen nib.

To apply calligraphic effects to your outline do this:

1. In the Outline Pen dialog box, from the **Calligraphy** area, set values for the **Stretch** and **Angle** of the calligraphic pen. (See Figure 8.10)

2. You can preview your settings in the **Nib shape** box. Figure 8.11 shows the difference seen in the outline with 3 sample settings.

3. Click **OK**.

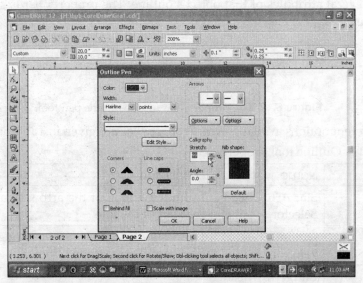

Figure 8.10 Choose a Stretch and Angle value for the calligraphic outline

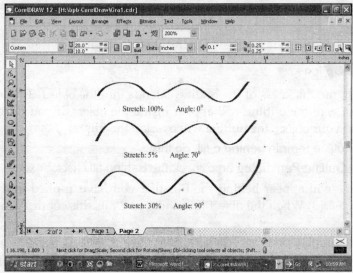

Figure 8.11 Curves with different Calligraphy settings

Setting Outline Options with the Property Bar

The property bar that appears when you select a curve object, enables you to define several attributes of that object's outline. The property bar is shown in the Figure 8.12.

Figure 8.12 The property bar for the outline pen tool

The different options available with Property Bar are given in Table 8.1.

Table 8.1   Outline tool property bar

Icon	Name	Description
	Star Arrowhead Selector	Defines the look of the arrow (if any) at the start of the line
	Outline Style Selector	Defines look of the outline ranging from dashes and dots to solid lines.
	End Arrowhead Selector	Defines the look of the arrow at the end of the curve
Hairline	Outline Width Selector	Enables you to pick from a larger set of outline widths similar to those available in the Outline flyout

Behind Fill Option

By default, the thickness of the outline extends into the object. That is, half of the thickness of the outline will appear inside the object. If you have applied any fills to your object, the outline will overlap the fills.

To make outline remain behind a fill, do this:

1.   In the Outline Pen dialog box, check the Behind fill check box.

The outline will appear behind the fills that you have applied in the object. (See Figure 8.13) When the object is without any fills this control produces no effect.

Scale with Image Option

By default, the outline width will not be set according to the size of the image For example, suppose you had set the outline width to 8-point thickness. Now if you decreased the object size by 50%, the thickness of your outline will still be 8-point. But you wanted the outline to be proportional to the size of the image.

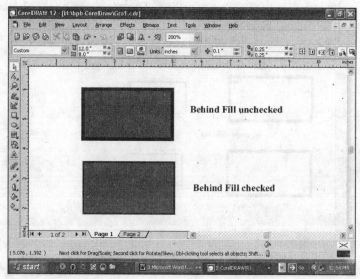

Figure 8.13 Illustrating behind fill option

To scale the outline proportional to image size, do this:

1. In the Outline Pen dialog box, check the Scale with Image check box.

Figure 8.14 shows the effect of decreasing size of object, on its outline, with Scaling the Image unchecked and checked.

Outline Color Dialog tool

Outline Color Dialog tool helps you in selecting or creating colors for your outlines, using color models, color palettes and color blends.

Fixed color palettes consist of some preset colors and are provided by third-party manufacturers. Some examples of these are PANTONE, HKS, and TRUMATCH. They are useful when your printer can handle only selected color palettes.

Custom color palettes can include colors from any color model or fixed color palette. Custom color palettes are saved as color palette files.

To choose a color using a color palette, do this:

1. Select the object.
2. Click the Outline tool flyout, and choose the Outline Color Dialog tool.
3. In the Outline Color dialog box, click on the Palette tab. The palette tab property sheet appears as in Figure 8.15.

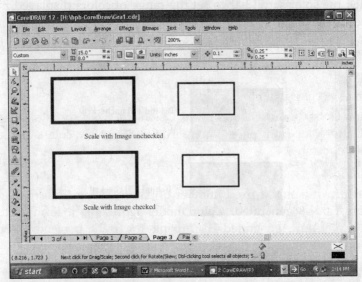

Figure 8.14 Scale with image illustrated

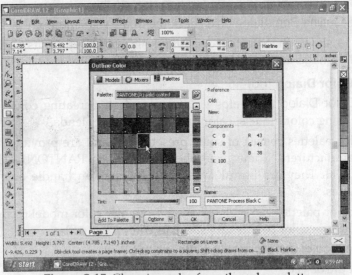

Figure 8.15 Choosing color from the color palette

4. Choose a fixed color palette from the **Palette** list box as seen in Figure 8.15.

5. Click the color scroll bar to set the range of colors displayed in the color selection area.

6. Click a color in the color selection area. Each color swatch on a fixed color palette is marked with a small white square.

7. Click Options and choose Show Color Names, to display or hide the names of color palettes.

8. Click Options and choose Swap Colors to swap the old to new colors. Select a color from palette area. The Old to New colors are seen in the Reference area.

Color Model

Palettes provide only a fixed number of colors. Using Color model, millions of colors can be generated. Color model represents a formula to produce colors. Colors are generated by mixing the right percentage of different colors.

A common color model is the CMYK color model. An exhaustive range of colors are produced by mixing right percentage of the colors namely, *cyan*, *magenta*, *yellow* and *black*.

Color viewers give a representation of a range of colors using one-dimensional or three-dimensional shapes.

To choose a color using a color viewer do this:

1. In the Outline Color dialog box, Click on the Models tab.

2. Choose a color model from the Model: drop down list box.

3. Click Options drop down list highlight Color viewers, and select a color viewer from sub menu. Figure 8.16 shows a CMY-3D Subtractive color viewer.

4. Click the color scroll bar at the right to set the range of colors displayed in the color selection area.

5. Click a color in the color selection area.

6. Drag the small square handles seen inside the viewer to the color of your choice. The color produced can be seen in the Reference area.

7. If the color you had created will be used frequently, click on the Add To Palette button. You can also provide a name for this color by typing a name in the Name list menu. The color will be added to the color palette located at the right of the drawing window.

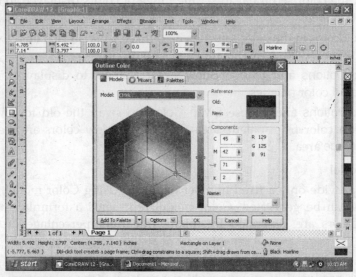

Figure 8.16 Choosing color using CMY-3D Subtractive model.

Color Harmonies

Color harmonies work by superimposing a shape, such as a rectangle or a triangle over a color wheel. Each vertical row in the color grid begins with the color located at one of the points on the superimposed shape.

The colors at opposite corners of the shape are always complementary, contrasting, or harmonious, depending on the shape you choose. The color harmonies are most useful when you are choosing several colors for a project.

To choose a color using color harmonies, do this:

1. In the Outline Color dialog box, click the Mixers tab.
2. Click Options, highlight Mixers and choose Color harmonies. (See Figure 8.17)
3. Choose a shape from the Hues list box. You will see the shape on the color wheel.
4. Choose an option from the Variation list box.
5. Drag the black dot on the color wheel.
6. Click a color swatch on the color palette below the color wheel.
7. When you have selected the color you want, Click OK.

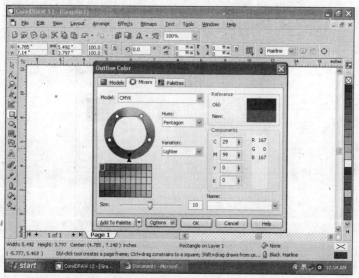

Figure 8.17 Choosing color using Color Harmonies

Color Blend

When you choose a color using color blends, you combine base colors to get the color you want. The color blender displays a grid of colors that it creates from the four base colors you choose

To choose a color using color blends, do this:

1. In the Outline Color dialog box, click the Mixers tab.
2. Click Options, highlight Mixers and choose Color blend.
3. Click on each of the color picker, and choose a color.
4. Click on a color in the color grid area. (See Figure 8.18)
5. You can change the cell size of the color grid by moving the Size slider.

Setting Outline Defaults

CorelDRAW by default creates outlines of 0.2 point width and of black color. You can change these default settings according to your wish and requirements.

To change CorelDRAW's default outlines for the current drawing, do this:

1. Without selecting any object, click the Outline tool flyout and choose Outline Pen Dialog.

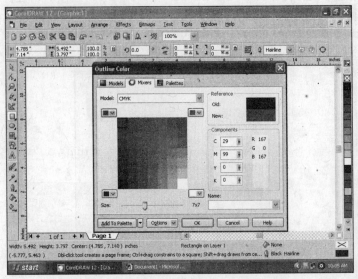

Figure 8.18 Choosing color using color blend

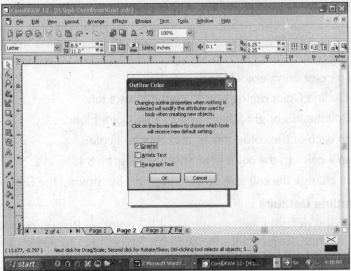

Figure 8.19 Click Ok to apply the outline settings to all the graphics in the current drawing.

2. A window as shown in Figure 8.19 will appear. Check against Graphics in the dialog box.

Now the settings that you do in the Outline Pen Dialog box will be applied to all the current drawings.

To change default outlines for all the documents, do this:

1. Click Tools menu and choose Options.

2. In the Options dialog box, click on the + symbol against Document. From the list under document choose Styles. (See Figure 8.20)

3. Click the Document.

4. Click the Edit button.

5. The Outline Pen Dialog box appears. Set the features that you want for all the documents you create thereafter.

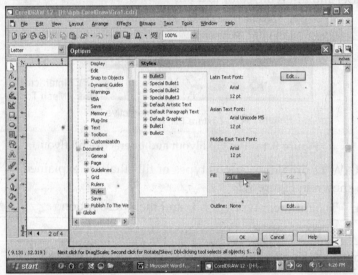

Figure 8.20 Click Edit... button to apply default settings to outline

CHAPTER 9

Fill Tool

Introduction

Any color, shade or pattern inside an object is taken as a Fill in CorelDRAW. The Interactive Fill Tool and the Fill Tool flyout will help you to fill the objects with every type of fills available. The Fill Flyout and the Interactive Fill flyout are shown in Figure 9.1. The Fill Color Dialog will help you in selecting the color model and applying color to a fill.

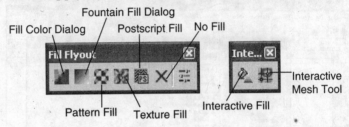

Figure 9.1 The Fill Flyout and Interactive fill flyout

CorelDRAW 12 provides various types of fills that are explained in Table 9.1 and also shown in Figure 9.2.

Table 9.1 The different types of fills and their description

Fill	Description
Uniform	A single color or shade that fills the entire object.
Fountain	A fountain fill is a smooth progression of two or more colors that adds depth to an object.
Patterns	An object is filled with a repeating pattern. The pattern can be a color or some bitmapped image.
Textures	Randomly generated fill that gives the object a natural look.
Mesh	Fill consisting of patches of color inside the object.

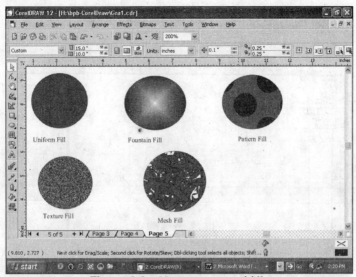

Figure 9.2 Various types of fills

Using Uniform Fills

Uniform fill consists of a single solid color filled inside an object. CorelDRAW 12 lets you add uniform fill to an object.

To apply a uniform fill, do this:

1. Select the object.

2. Click the Interactive Fill flyout and choose the Interactive Fill tool.

3. In the property bar, click on the Fill type list box, and choose Uniform Fill. (See Figure 9.3).

4. You can also fill an object by clicking on a color on the color palette, located at the right of the drawing window.

5. To mix colors, hold Ctrl key and click on the colors in the color palette.

Using Fountain Fills

In Fountain fills, the colors or shades gradually change inside the object. There are four types of fountain fills: *linear, radial, conical* and *square*. (See Figure 9.4).

Linear fountain fills flows in a straight line across the object. Conical fountain fills circles from the center of the object. A radial fountain fill radiates from the center of the object. A square fountain fill is dispersed in concentric squares from the center of the object.

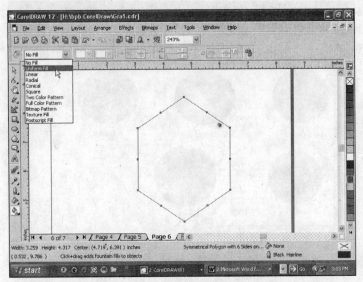

Figure 9.3 Choosing Uniform fill for the selected object

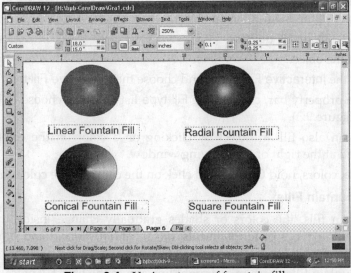

Figure 9.4 Various types of fountain fills

You can apply preset fountain fills, two-color fountain fills or custom fountain fills to an object. You can also specify the attributes for the fountain fill like direction, angle, centre point etc.

To apply a preset fountain fill, do this:

1. Select the object.
2. Click the Fill flyout, and choose the Fountain Fill Dialog. Fountain Fill dialog box appears as shown in Figure 9.5.
3. In the Fountain Fill dialog box, click the Type: list box, and choose a fountain fill (See Figure 9.5).

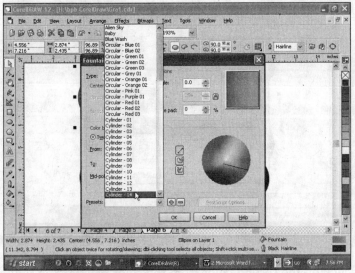

Figure 9.5   Choosing a preset fountain fill

4. Click on the Presets list box and choose a fill.
5. You can see the preview in the box at the top right corner of the dialog box.

Custom fountain fills can contain two or more colors, which you can position anywhere in the fill's progression

To apply a custom fountain fill, do this:

1. Select the object.
2. Click the Fill flyout, and choose the Fountain Fill Dialog.
3. In the Fountain Fill dialog box, click the Type list box, and choose a fountain fill.
4. Click on the Custom radio button.
5. Choose a color from the color palette. If the color of your choice is not available in the current palette, click on the Others button.

6. To set the angle of this color, either choose a value from the Angle: list box or click on the box above the color palette.

7. To set the position of the second color, drag the slider located above the box at the left of color palette (See Figure 9.6).

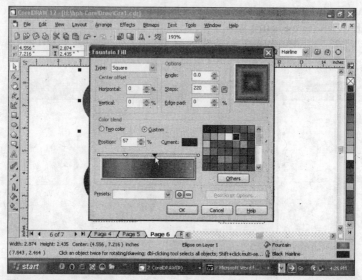

Figure 9.6 Dragging the slider to adjust the position of the color

8. Now click on the second color from the color palette. You will observe a smooth transition of one color into another.

9. To add more than two colors, double click on the area in between the two colors and choose color from the color palette.

10. To set the number of bands used to display the transition from one color to another, click on the small button to the right of Steps: list box, and type a value in the list.

11. To change a color, click the pointer seen above the color band you want to change and choose a color.

12. To delete a color, double click on the pointer seen above the color band you want to delete.

13. To save the fill created by you click press the + button and type a name in the Presets: box.

14. Click OK.

Using Texture Fills

CorelDRAW 12 provides several preset textures for you to fill objects. Each texture has a set of attributes that can be changed as per your need. You can use colors from any color model or palette to customize these texture fills.

To apply texture fills, do this:

1. Select an object.
2. Click the Fill flyout and choose the Texture Fill Dialog button. The dialog box appears as in Figure 9.7.

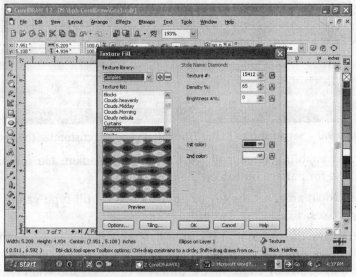

Figure 9.7   The Texture Fill dialog box

3. In the Texture Fill dialog box, choose a texture library from the Texture library: list box.
4. Choose a texture from the Texture list: box. You can see the preview also.
5. If you want to create a new texture, specify the texture attributes you want in the Style Name area.
6. To change the size of texture tiles, Click Tiling... . The Tiling dialog box appears as shown in Figure 9.8.
7. Type values in the Width: and Height: boxes. *Alternatively*, the size of texture tiles can be changed by selecting the object using Interactive fill

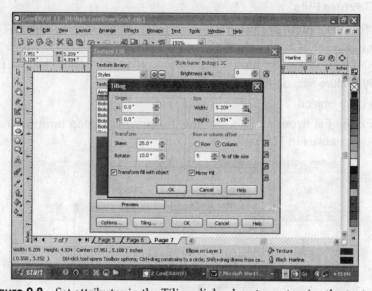

Figure 9.8   Set attributes in the Tiling dialog box to customize the texture

tool and enabling the Small tile for pattern, Medium tile for pattern or Large tile for pattern button on the property bar.

8. In the Origin area, set the tile origin of a texture fill type values in the x: and y: boxes.

9. To offset the tile origin of a texture fill, enable the Row or Column option and type an amount of offset in the % of tile size box. The difference in effect that occurs by choosing the different offsets is shown in Figure 9.9.

10. To rotate a texture fill, type a value in the Rotate: box.

11. To skew a texture fill, type a value in the Skew: box.

12. To mirror a texture fill, enable the Mirror fill check box.

13. You can save this custom texture you created for future use. Click Add and type a name for the fill in the Texture library list box.

14. To further set the tiling options, click the Options... button. An Options dialog box appears as shown in Figure 9.10. Type a value in the Bitmap resolution list box. Set Maximum tile width you want in the Maximum tile width list box. To reset the default values for width and resolution, click on the Reset button.

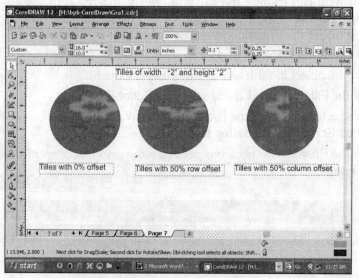

Figure 9.9 The effect of different offset of tiles

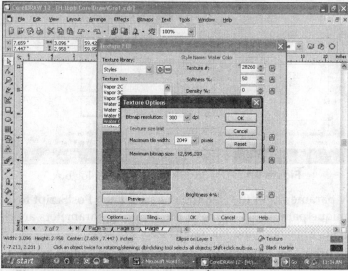

Figure 9.10 The Options dialog box for the Texture settings

Using PostScript fills

PostScript texture fills are micro programs designed using PostScript language. You cannot customize PostScript fills as you do with other fill types. But you can change the existing ones using the controls given in the PostScript Texture dialog. You can view PostScript fills only if you are viewing it under the Enhanced View or Normal View

To apply PostScript texture fills, do this:

1. Select the object to which you want to apply the fill.
2. Click the Fill flyout and choose the PostScript Fill Dialog.
3. Choose a texture from the list of textures available in the box at the left of the PostScript Texture dialog box.
4. Click the Preview fill check box on to see the preview of each of the texture (See Figure 9.11).

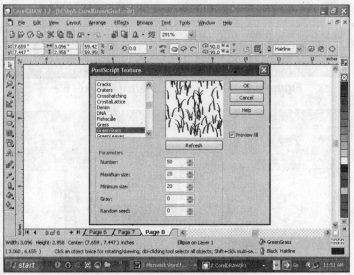

Figure 9.11 The PostScript Texture dialog box.

5. Specify parameters in the Parameters area. Each PostScript texture has its own unique parameters. Some of the common parameters are Frequency, Line width, Maximum and Minimum size.

After setting the new parameters, click the Refresh button to apply the new settings. *Alternatively*, you can apply PostScript texture fills from the Property Bar.

To apply PostScript texture fill from the Property bar, do this:

1. Select the object.

2. Click the Interactive Fill flyout, and choose the Interactive fill tool.

3. Choose PostScript fill from the Fill type list box on the property bar.

4. Choose a PostScript fill from the PostScript fill textures list box as shown in Figure 9.12.

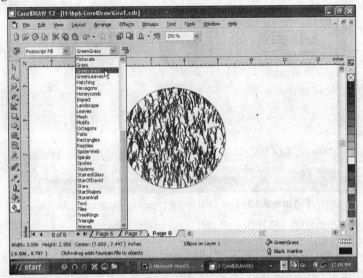

Figure 9.12 Choosing a PostScript fill from the PostScript fill textures list box

5. To change the chosen fill's parameters, click the Edit fill button. The PostScript Texture dialog box of Figure 9.12 appears. Specify the settings like frequency, line width etc. and click OK.

Using Pattern fills

Pattern fills are used to fill the entire object with repeating patterns. You can fill objects with various Pattern tiles. Patterns can be two-color, full-color or bitmapped pattern fills. Figure 9.13 illustrates the different types of fills available.

- A two-color pattern fill is composed of only two colors that you choose.

- A full color pattern fill consists of lines and fills.

- A bit mapped pattern fill is a bitmapped image whose complexity is determined by its size, image resolution and its bit depth. Bitmap patterns allow you to place complex photographs or other images within an object.

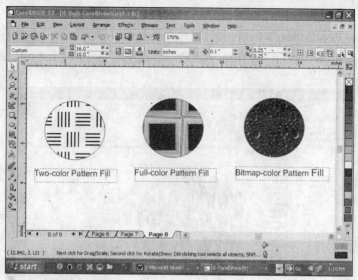

Figure 9.13 The Different types of Pattern Fills

To apply a pattern fill, do this:

1. Select the object.
2. Click the Fill Tool flyout, and choose Pattern Fill Dialog button. A dialog box appears as shown in Figure 9.14.

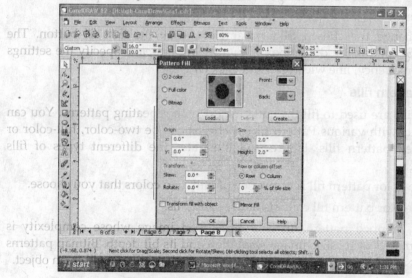

Figure 9.14 The Pattern Fill dialog box

3. In the **Pattern Fill** dialog box, Click on **2 color**, **Full color** or **Bitmap** radio button.

4. Click the drop down list to the right of the dialog box, and choose a pattern (See Figure 9.15).

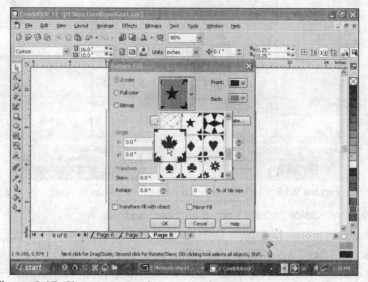

Figure 9.15 Choosing a 2 color pattern from the Pattern Fill dialog box

5. To import any pattern saved in your hard disk, Click on the **Load** button and locate the image in the **Import** dialog box.

6. Click the **Front** color picker and choose a color for the front design.

7. Click the **Back** color picker and choose a color for the background.

8. Click on the **Create...** button to create a two-color pattern fill.

9. In the **Pattern Editor** dialog box (See Figure 9.16), choose a resolution for the Edit grid in the **Bitmap size** area. For example, choosing 16 x 16, makes the Edit grid to contain 16 x 16 squares.

10. In the **Pen size** area, choose a pen size. For example, choosing 2 x 2 size changes pen size to a **2 x 2** square.

11. Click on the grid pattern to create a pattern of your choice. You will observe that cells are added on as you click.

12. To delete a cell right click on it.

You can also create pattern out of any graphic of your choice.

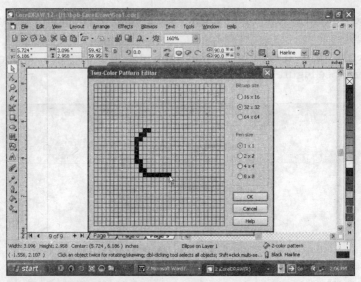

Figure 9.16 Click on the grid pattern to create the pattern

To create a two-color pattern from a graphic, do this:

1. Click Tools menu, highlight Create and choose Pattern.
2. Click on either Two color or Full color radio button.
3. In the Resolution area, click on a resolution type you want (See Figure 9.17).
4. Click OK and then marquee select the graphic or area of the graphic.

To create a full-color pattern from a graphic, do this:

1. Click Tools menu, highlight Create and choose Pattern.
2. Click on the Full color radio button.
3. Click OK and marquee select the graphic or area of the graphic you want. (See Figure 9.18).
4. The Save Vector Pattern dialog box appears. Save the pattern in the location of your choice.

Using Mesh fills

Mesh fills consists of patches of colors. When the mesh fill is applied, many nodes appear inside the object in the form of rows and columns. The number of rows and columns can be set by you. You can then drag and move these nodes to a new position. To apply a color, select a part of mesh, press Ctrl, key and click a color from the color palette. The effect is felt when the

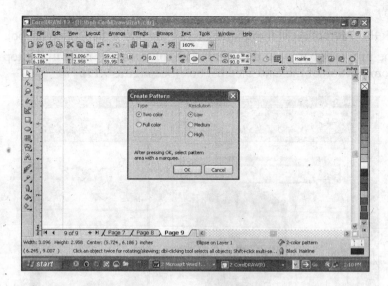

Figure 9.17 Dialog box to create a pattern from a graphic

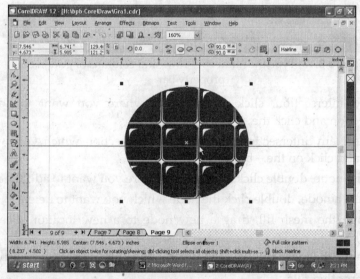

Figure 9.18 Marquee selecting the graphic area for saving it as a pattern

object is filled with more than one color. You will observe how the colors blend together and form patches to create a pattern.

To apply a mesh fill to an object, do this:

1. Select the object.

2. Click the Interactive fill flyout and choose the Interactive mesh fill tool.

3. In the property bar, type the number of columns and rows in the top and bottom portion of the Grid Size list box (See Figure 9.19).

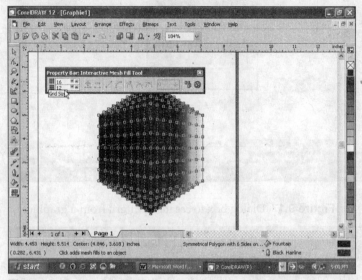

Figure 9.19 Type the number of rows and columns of grid in the property bar

4. To add intersection, click at the point where you want to add the intersection and click the + button.

5. To delete any intersection, click on the intersection which you want to delete and click on the – button.

6. To add a node, double click at the point where you want to add the node.

7. To delete a node, double click the node which you want to delete.

8. To shape the mesh fill, drag a new node to a new location (See Figure 9.20).

9. To remove the mesh fill, click the Clear mesh button on the property bar.

Using Interactive fills

With the Interactive fill flyout, the fill patterns are not modified or created in the dialog box. Rather, all the settings that need to be selected or changed are available in the Property Bar. Thus, instead of making changes to fills in a small preview window, you can experiment with fills directly on the object and change accordingly.

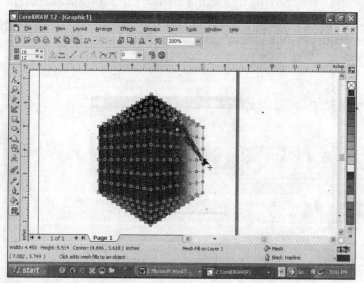

Figure 9.20 Changing the position of color or the direction of color flow

To apply interactive fills, do this:

1. Select the object.
2. Click the Interactive fill flyout and choose the Interactive fill tool.
3. From the property bar, choose the type of fill you want for the object.
4. Set the attributes of the fill from the property bar itself.

You will observe that you are able to apply most of the fill patterns without having to use dialog boxes.

Copying fills

You can copy the fills applied to an object to another object.

To copy fills, do this:

1. Click the Pick tool.
2. Select the object from which the fill is to be copied.
3. Click the Edit menu and choose Copy Properties From.
4. Check the Fill check box (See Figure 9.21).
5. Click and then click on the object to which the fill need to be copied.

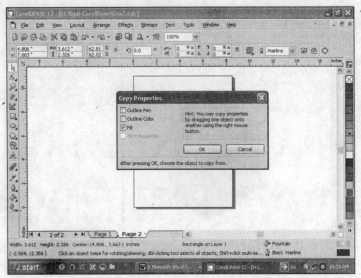

Figure 9.21 Click OK to copy the fills to another object

Setting Fill Defaults

You can change default fill settings to the one you like.

To change CorelDRAW's default fill settings for the current drawing, do this:

1. Without selecting any object, Click the Fill tool flyout and choose Fill Color Dialog button.

2. A Uniform Fill dialog box appears as shown in Figure 9.22. Check against Graphics in the dialog box.

3. Now the settings that you do in the Fill Color Dialog box will be applied to all the current drawings.

To change CorelDRAW's default fills for all the documents, do this:

1. Click Tools menu and choose Options.

2. In the Options dialog box, click on the + symbol against Document.

3. From the list under document choose Styles (See Figure.9.23).

4. Choose a fill type from the Fill: type list box.

5. Click on the Edit button.

6. Set the features that you want to, for all your documents. These changes will become default settings for the fills thereafter.

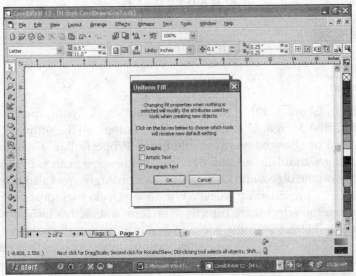

Figure 9.22 Click ok to apply the fill settings.

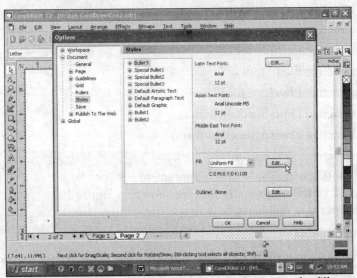

Figure 9.23 Click on Edit to create default settings for fills

CHAPTER 10

Interactive Tools

Introduction

You learnt in Chapter 9 that using the Interactive fill flyout, the fill patterns are not modified or created in the dialog box. Rather, all the settings that need to be selected or changed are available in the Property Bar. Thus, instead of making changes to fills in a small preview window, you can experiment with fills directly on the object and change them accordingly. You also learnt about the interactivity provided by Docker Windows. Docker windows help you to apply and see the effect there directly. The term interactive indicates that the user is able to interact with the package and can instruct the package to make the changes. CorelDRAW 12 provides various other tools called interactive tools for this purpose. These interactive tools are:

- Interactive Fill tool
- Interactive Mesh Fill tool
- Interactive Distortion tool
- Interactive Extrude tool
- Interactive Blend tool
- Interactive Envelope tool
- Interactive Drop Shadow tool
- Interactive Transparency tool and
- Interactive Contour tool

All these tools are available in the Interactive Fill Tool flyout as well as in the Interactive flyout. Both these flyouts are shown in Figure 10.1.

In this Chapter you will learn how to use these interactive tools.

Distorting Objects

The Interactive distortion tool lets you apply a *Push* or *Pull* distortion, a *Zipper* distortion, or *a Twister distortion* to an object.

- The Push or Pull Distortion lets you push the edges of an object in or pull the edges out of the object.
- The Zipper distortion lets you apply a saw tooth like edge to the object.

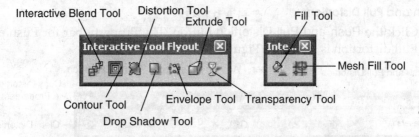

Interactive Blend Tool   Distortion Tool   Fill Tool
                          Extrude Tool

                                                    Mesh Fill Tool

Contour Tool   Envelope Tool Transparency Tool

Drop Shadow Tool

Figure 10.1 The Interactive fill flyout and the Interactive flyout

- The Twister distortion twists the object. The direction and degree of twist can be adjusted according to your will.

Figure 10.2 shows the effect of applying these three distortions on a rectangle.

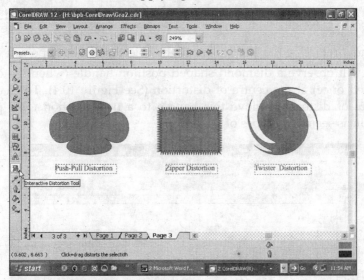

Figure 10.2 Effect of different distortions on a rectangle

To distort an object, do this:

1. Select the object which is to be distorted.

2. Click the Interactive flyout and choose the Interactive Distortion Tool.

3. In the property bar, click on the Push and Pull Distortion, Zipper Distortion or Twister Distortion button as the case may be.

Push and Pull Distortion

1. Click the **Push and Pull Distortion** button. The Property bar for Push and Pull distortion is shown in Figure 10.3.

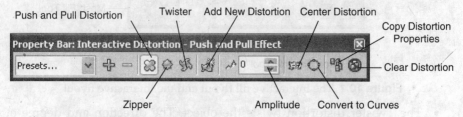

Push and Pull Distortion   Twister   Add New Distortion   Center Distortion

Copy Distortion Properties

Clear Distortion

Zipper   Amplitude   Convert to Curves

Figure 10.3 Interactive Distortion Property bar

2. You can select a preset distortion from the **Preset** drop down list.

3. *Alternatively*, click on the object where you want the centre of distortion to be placed.

4. Without releasing mouse, drag until the object is of the shape you wanted.

5. You will observe a diamond shaped position handle (when the object is clicked once) at the centre of distortion (See Figure 10.4). To change the centre of distortion, move this handle to a new location. This position handle is seen in all types of distortions.

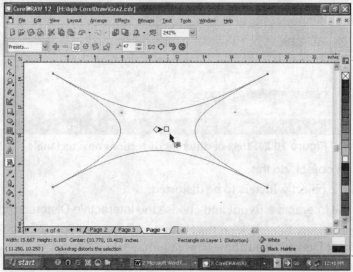

Figure 10.4 The position handle at the centre of the rectangle

Copy Distortion

1. Select the object to which you want to copy a distortion.
2. Click Effects menu choose Copy effect and select Distortion from.
3. Click a distorted object. See Figure 10.5
4. *Alternatively*, you can use the Eyedropper tool to copy the effect.

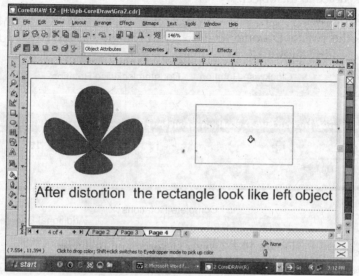

Figure 10.5 Copy Distortion to another object

Zipper Distortion

1. Click the Zipper Distortion button in the property bar. The Property bar for Zipper distortion is shown in Figure 10.6.

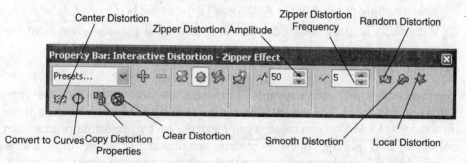

Figure 10.6 Zipper Distortion property bar

2. You can choose from preset zipper distortion listed in the **Preset List:** list box.

3. Specify the frequency and amplitude of the distortion in the **Zipper Distortion Amplitude** and **Zipper Distortion Frequency** list box.

4. *Alternatively*, drag the nodes of the object to apply a zipper distortion of your choice to the object.

Twister Distortion

1. Click the **Twister Distortion** button. The property bar for Twister distortion is shown in Figure 10.7.

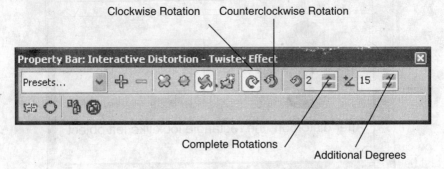

Figure 10.7 Twister Distortion property bar

2. You can choose from preset twister distortions given in the **Preset List** list box.

3. Specify the direction of twist by clicking on the **Clockwise Rotation** or **Counterclockwise Rotation** button.

4. Now specify the number of twists in the **Complete Rotations** list box.

5. Specify angle of twist in the **Additional Degrees** list box.

6. *Alternatively*, drag the nodes of the object, until the distortion is of the shape you desire.

Extruding Objects

You can add a 3-D effect to an object using the **Interactive Extrude Tool**. Extrusion combines 3-D effects with shadows and the object inherits a three dimensional look. You can create vector extrusions by projecting points from an object and joining them to create an illusion of three dimensions. CorelDRAW 12 also lets you apply a vector extrusion to an object in a group. You can change an extruded form by rotating it and rounding its corners.

To extrude an object, do this:

1. Select the object which is to be extruded.

2. Click the Interactive flyout and choose Interactive Extrude Tool. The property bar provides a wide variety of options for extrusion. The options available in property bar are explained here. Figure 10.8 shows the property bar for Interactive Extrude tool.

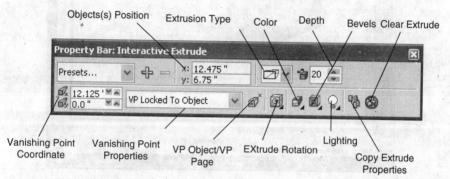

Figure 10.8 The Interactive Extrude property bar

3. You can choose from a list of predefined extrusions available in the Preset List list box.

4. Drag the object's selection handles to set the direction and depth of the extrusion. Figure 10.9 shows the object being extruded in bottom right direction.

5. You can also specify object's horizontal and vertical position in the x: and y: box respectively. Experiment with other options available in the Property bar and observe the effects for yourself.

6. Select the Extrusion type, from the drop down list.

7. To rotate an extrusion, Select an extruded object. Click the Extrude rotation button on the property bar. Drag the extrusion in the direction you want.

8. Click the Color button and choose a color for selected object. You also have the option of bringing the extrusion effect using color shading. If you choose Use Color Shading, specify a color in the From: and To: drop down color palette (See Figure 10.10). In this case, the extrusion effect starts from the color you choose in the From: list and ends in the color you choose in the To: list.

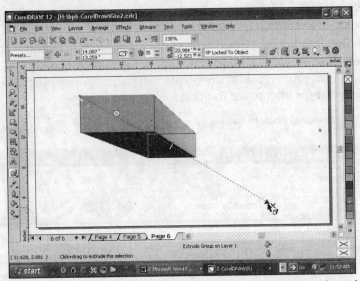

Figure 10.9 Extruding the object with the Interactive extrude tool

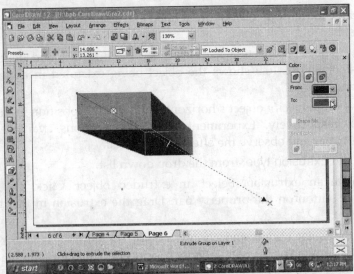

Figure 10.10 Selecting color type for the extrusion.

9. Select an extruded object. Click the Bevels button on the property bar. Enable the Use bevel check box. Type a value in the Bevel depth box and Bevel angle box as seen in Figure 10.11.

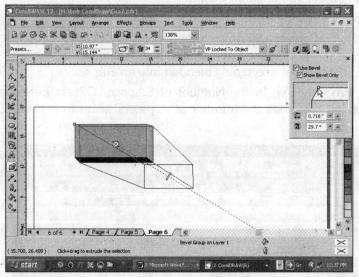

Figure 10.11   To showing Bevels using and hide the extrusion

10. You can also set the bevel depth and angle by using the Interactive display box in the bevel list box. You can show only the bevel and hide the extrusion by enabling the Show bevel only check box. (See Figure 10.11)

11. To add some lighting to the object, click the Lighting button and choose a light number and intensity. The effect on the object is felt accordingly.

12. To copy Extrude properties to another object .

   • Select the object you want to extrude.

   • Click the Effect menu and choose either Copy effect or Clone effect, select the Extrude From... you will see the black arrow, click the extruded object, then you will feel the effect of the object.

13. To remove a vector extrusion by clicking the Clear extrude button on the property bar.

Blending Objects

Blending one object to another means, filling the space between the two objects with intermediary objects. CorelDRAW lets you blend one object to another. These intermediary objects illustrate a step by step transition from the first object to the second object. The transition is not only in size and shape but in color also. You can also define a path for the blend.

To blend an object into another, do this:

1. Click the Interactive flyout and choose Interactive Blend Tool.

2. Click the first object and drag to the second object. When you release the mouse, you will observe intermediate objects connecting the two objects. Figure 10.12 shows a rectangle blended into an ellipse.

3. In the Property bar, in the **Number of Steps or Offsets between Blend Shapes** list box, fixes the number of steps you want in between the two objects.

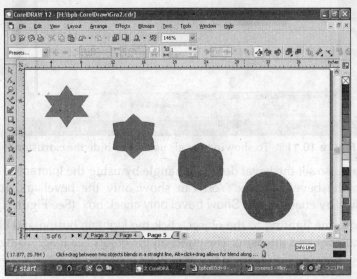

Figure 10.12 The Start being blended into an circle with two intermediate steps.

4. To blend along a predefined path, draw a curve (the path). Then click on the Path Properties button and choose New Path.

5. Now point to the curve as shown in Figure 10.13.

6. You will observe that the original objects and the intermediary objects align themselves on the curve (See Figure 10.14).

If you change the size, shape, color or any other characteristics of the original objects, the characteristics of the intermediate objects will change automatically.

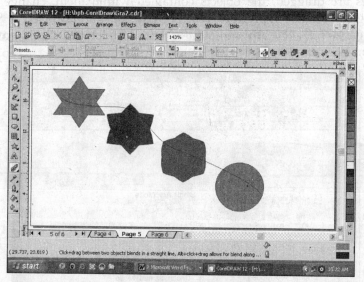

Figure 10.13 Pointing to the curve that will define the path for the blend

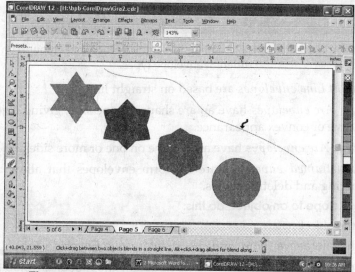

Figure 10.14 The blend follows the path of the curve.

Interactive Envelopes

You can confine objects in frames called envelopes. When nodes of these envelopes are dragged, the objects contained within them, change shapes accordingly. You can apply four types of envelopes to an object – *Straight Line*, *Single Arc*, *Double Arc* and *Unconstrained* Envelopes. These envelopes are shown in Figure 10.15.

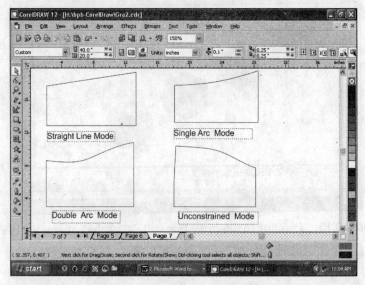

Figure 10.15   Effect of dragging (in same direction and amount) on different envelope types.

- *Straight Line envelopes* are based on straight lines.
- *Single Arc envelopes* have an arc shape on one side, giving objects the concave or convex appearance.
- *Double Arc envelopes* have an S shape on one or more sides.
- *Unconstrained envelopes* are freeform envelopes that allow adding, changing and deleting nodes.

To apply envelope to an object, do this:

1. Select the object
2. Click the Interactive flyout and choose Interactive Envelope Tool.
3. In the property bar, click on Envelope straight line mode, Envelope Single arc Mode, Envelope Double arc Mode or Envelope Unconstrained Mode button, depending on which type of envelope you need. Figure 10.16 shows the property bar for the Interactive Envelope Tool.

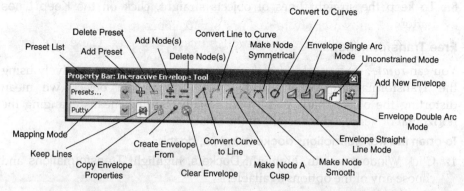

Figure 10.16   Interactive Envelope Tool property bar.

4. Pull, push or drag the nodes of the envelope until the object is of the shape you desire (See Figure 10.17).

Figure 10.17   The "BEST" text has been modified inside an envelope

5. You can also apply a preset envelope to an object by choosing one from the Preset List list box.

6. To add envelope to an object that is already enveloped, click on the Add New Envelope button.

7. To remove envelope, click Effects menu and choose Clear Envelope.

8. To keep the straight lines of objects straight, click on the **Keep Lines** button.

Free Transformations

You can *rotate*, *skew*, *scale*, *stretch* and *position* an object interactively using the Transformation Docker window. By skewing an object, we mean distorting the object shape non-proportionally. Scaling means changing the horizontal or vertical dimensions of the object.

To open the Transformations docker window, do this:

1. Click <u>W</u>indows menu, highlight Dockers, highlight Transformations and choose any of the options available.

2. The Transformation Docker window appears as shown in Figure 10.18.

To rotate an object, do this:

1. Select the object which is to be rotated

2. In the docker window click the **Rotate** button (See Figure 10.18).

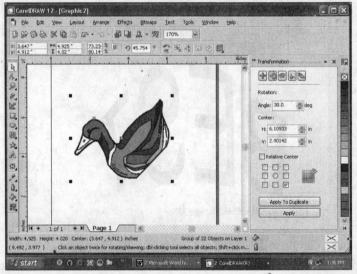

Figure 10.18   Figure rotated through the Rotate Transformation Docker window

3. Click any of the checkboxes below the **Relative center** check box, to specify the position around which the object is to be rotated.

4. Type the angle through which the object is to be rotated in the **Angle** list box.

5. Specify the horizontal and vertical coordinates around which you want to rotate the object in the H and V list box respectively.

6. Click Apply

To scale an object, do this:

1. Select the object

2. Click the Scale and Mirror button (See Figure 10.19).

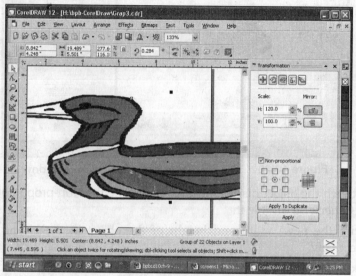

Figure 10.19   Figure scaled and flipped horizontally.

3. In the H and V list boxes, specify the percentage by which you want to scale horizontally and vertically the object.

4. Click on the Horizontal Mirror button to flip the object horizontally i.e. left to right and vice versa.

5. Click on the Vertical Mirror button to flip the object vertically i.e. top to bottom and vice versa.

6. Click Apply.

To stretch the object, do this:

1. Select the object.

2. Click on the Size button (See Figure 10.20).

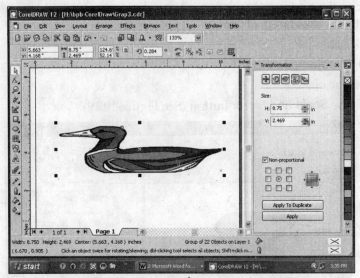

Figure 10.20   The Size Transformation Docker window

3. To stretch the object disproportionably, enable the Non-proportional check box. Otherwise disable it.

4. Specify the new width and height of the object in the H and V boxes respectively.

5. Click Apply.

To skew an object, do this:

1. Select the object which is to be skewed.

2. Click the Skew button (See Figure 10.21).

3. Specify the number of degrees by which you want to skew the object horizontally and vertically in the H and V list boxes respectively.

4. Click Apply.

To position an object in a new location, do this:

1. Select the object.

2. Click on the Positions button.

3. Disable the Relative position check box.

4. Specify the horizontal and vertical position of the object in the H and V boxes respectively.

5. Click Apply.

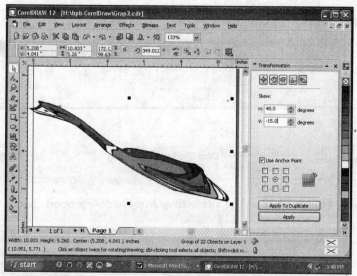

Figure 10.21   Figure skewed through the Skew Transformation
Docker window

6. To close the docker window, click the close button on the window. When you select an object with pick tool, the transformation features are available in the property bar. You can apply rotation, skewing, scaling and sizing transformations to the object through this property bar.

Applying Interactive Shadow

Adding a shadow to an object gives an illusion of depth or third dimension to an object. The object attains a three dimensional view if shadow is added to it. The Interactive Drop Shadow Tool allows you to add shadow on an object.

To apply shadow on an object, do this:

1. Select the object.
2. Click the Interactive flyout and choose Interactive Drop Shadow Tool. Figure 10.22 shows the property bar for Interactive Drop Shadow Tool.
3. Click on the object.
4. Drag and draw a shadow around the object. At first it appears as a wire frame duplicate of the object (See Figure 10.23)
5. *Alternatively,* you can also select a preset shadow style from the Preset List list box.

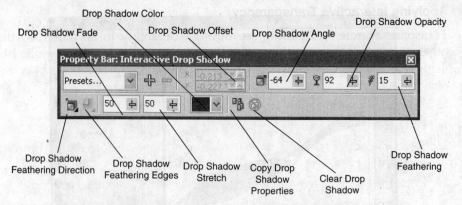

Figure 10.22 The Interactive Drop Shadow property bar.

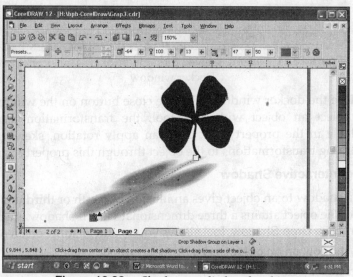

Figure 10.23 Shadow applied to the object

6. Choose a color for the shadow from the Drop Shadow Color drop down list.

7. Specify Angle of shadow and its opacity in the Drop Shadow Angle and Drop Shadow Opacity slider respectively. Opacity refers to the inability to see through the shadow.

8. If you want to adjust the level of sharpness along the edges of the shadow, specify the value in the Drop Shadow Feathering slider.

Applying Interactive Transparency

Transparency refers to adding see through capability to an object, so that other objects can be seen through it. Interactive transparency is applied by using the Interactive Transparency Tool. Transparency is applied on one object and then this object is placed on another object.

To apply transparency to an object, do this:

1. Drag and place the first object over the second object.
2. Select the object which is to be made transparent (the object that is on the front side).
3. Click the Interactive flyout and choose Interactive Transparency Tool.
4. Click and drag on the object from the point where you want minimum transparency to the point where you want maximum transparency (See Figure 10.24.
5. You will now be able to see the second object through the first object. Figure 10.24 shows the effect of applying transparency to an object.

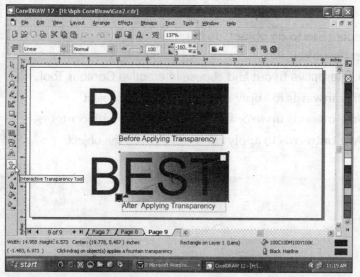

Figure 10.24   Transparent rectangle made the text behind it to be visible

Applying Interactive Contours

Contours are concentric lines drawn inside or outside an object. With CorelDRAW 12, you can draw contours to inside, to outside and to center of the object. Figure 10.25 depicts these three contours.

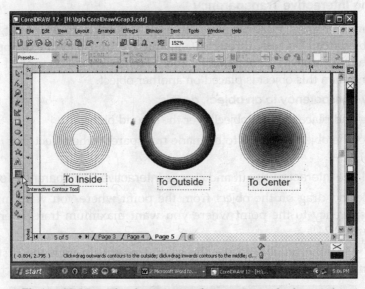

Figure 10.25   The three types of contours applied to circles

To apply contours to an object, do this:

1. Select the object
2. Click Interactive flyout and choose Interactive Contour Tool.

    -   Drag inwards to apply contours inside the object.
    -   Drag inwards up to centre to fill the object with contours.
    -   Drag outwards to apply contours outside the object.

CHAPTER 11

Working with Images

Introduction

In this Chapter, you will learn to import and export an image, as well as how to modify or manipulate them. You must have got an idea by now that CorelDRAW 12 works fine with Vector images. But CorelDRAW 12 is also capable of working on bitmap images, wherein the images are created in the form of dots, better known as pixels. In addition, CorelDRAW 12 comes packaged with Corel PHOTO-PAINT, a powerful program for creating and editing bitmap images.

Image Formats

You may have read about various image formats like *GIF, JPG, TIFF, EPS,* etc. An image format defines how application package stores information in a file. CorelDRAW 12 images are stored in *CDR* format and Bitmap images are stored in *BMP* format. The image format is identified by the three letter extension appended at the end of a filename. This filename extension helps you to identify. The computer also differentiates among different types of files or file formats using the extensions.

If you want to use an image created in a different application package, then you need to import that file to be read by your package. Similarly, if you created an image in CorelDRAW 12, but you want to use it in another application, you must export the file to a different file format readable by that package.

Importing Images

One way to insert an image into the drawing window of CorelDRAW 12 is to import it. Thus, an already existing image is first imported into CorelDRAW and then processed or manipulated. When an image is imported into CorelDRAW 12, it will get converted into a vector graphics.

To import an image, do this:

1. Click File menu and choose Import....
2. In the Import dialog box, choose the folder where the image is stored from the Look in: drop down menu (See Figure 11.1).
3. Select the image format from the Files of Type:.

Figure 11.1 The Import dialog box.

4. Enable the Preview check box. If this check box is enabled, you can see a small preview of the image in the box.

5. Click OK.

6. Point to the location where you want to place the image and click there. Image will be placed at this location.

Using the Scrapbook

CorelDRAW 12 provides a Scrapbook consisting of ready made images. It is available in the form of a docker window.

Note: Scrapbook helps in organizing and accessing your favorite elements. The images that you feel will be used frequently, can be stored in the Scrapbook.

To work with Scrapbook, do this:

1. Click Tools menu, highlight Scrapbook and choose Browse.

2. The Scrapbook docker window appears as shown in Figure 11.2.

3. Double click the icon of the directory, which contains the images you want. *Alternatively*, choose the folder from the Go to for a different folder using drop down menu.

4. When you have located your image, drag the image into the drawing window (See Figure 11.3). Keep the docker window open while you work.

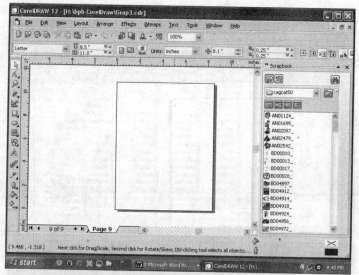

Figure 11.2 The Scrapbook Docker Window

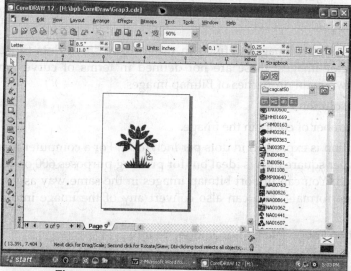

Figure 11.3 Image dragged from Scrapbook

5. Click on the **Content on Web** button to search online, any web site for photos, sound etc.

6. Click the **Search** button to search for any drawing using a keyword. Type the keyword in the **Search for:** text area (See Figure 11.4).

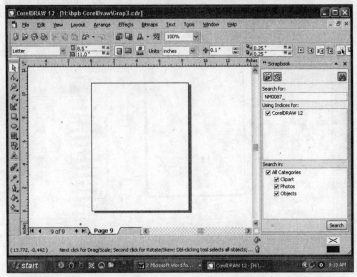

Figure 11.4 Type the image name in the Search for: area.

Bitmap Images

Bitmap images are images defined in the form of small dots called pixels. Unlike Vector images, these are not defined in terms of curves and lines. There are two main properties of Bitmap images.

- Resolution
- Number of colors in the image.

The resolution is expressed in dots per inch (dpi). For a computer monitor, 72 (dpi) dots per square inch is ideal but for printing purposes 600 or 1200 dpi is widely used. You can import bitmap images in the same way as you import other image formats. You can also convert any of the image into a bitmap image.

To convert an image into bitmap image, do this:

1. Select the image which is to be converted.
2. Click Bitmaps menu and choose Convert to Bitmap....
3. The Convert to Bitmap dialog box appears as in Figure 11.5.
4. In the dialog box, choose a color mode from the Color: drop down menu.
5. Specify a resolution of your choice in the Resolution: list box.
6. To eliminate jagged edges in the image disable the Anti aliasing check box.

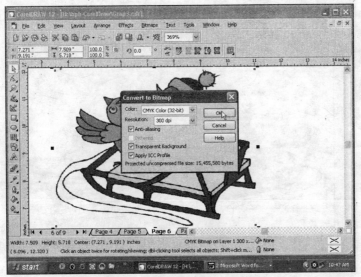

Figure 11.5 Convert to Bitmap dialog box.

7. To eliminate any colored background in the image, check the Transparent Background check box.

8. Click OK

Cropping Bitmap Image

Cropping a bitmap image means cutting it short. In other words cropping an image means trimming an image.

To crop a bitmap image, do this:

1. Select the image

2. Click Shape flyout and choose Shape Tool.

3. Drag inwards the nodes of the image in the direction in which you want to crop (See Figure 11.6).

4. Now if you reverse the process you can get back the whole image. If you want to completely remove the cropped part, click Bitmaps menu and choose Crop Bitmap.

Bitmap Special Effects

You can apply a range of useful effects to bitmap images. These effects are Color masking i.e. removing a selected color from the image, transforming

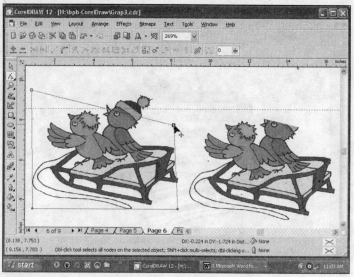

Figure 11.6 Node dragged in with the shape tool (right). Image after being cropped (left)

color, applying contour, etc. Most of these effects are available in the Bitmap menu. Some of them are explained here.

To apply 3D effects, do this:

1. Select the image.

2. Click **Bitmaps** menu, highlight **3D Effects** and choose the effect that you want to apply (See Figure 11.7).

3. As an Example, choose **Emboss**. **Emboss** dialog box appears as seen in Figure 11.8.

4. Slide the **Depth:** and the **Level:** slider to specify the emboss depth and level.

5. Also specify the angle at which light hits the engraving in the **Direction:** list box.

6. Choose an embossing color from the **Emboss color** area. Use the eyedropper button to select a color from outside the dialog box.

7. Click the preview button to preview the image.

8. Click OK (See Figure 11.9).

To apply Art Strokes, do this:

1. Select the image.

Figure 11.7 The different 3D Effects for Bitmap Images

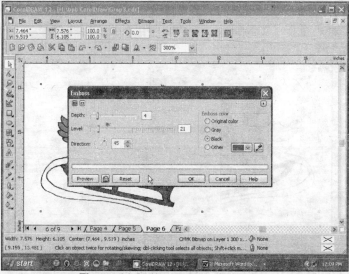

Figure 11.8 The Emboss dialog box

2. Click **B**itmaps menu, highlight **A**rt Strokes and choose from any of the available strokes (See Figure 11.10).

3. As an example, choose **P**astels.

Figure 11.9 Embossed Image

Figure 11.10 Different Art Stroke Effects for Bitmap Images

4. In the Pastel Type area, choose Soft for a soft pastel or choose Oil for a smudged pastel.

5. Slide the slider of the Stroke size: to set the size of brushstroke.

6. Set the color variations of brushstrokes in the Hue Variation: area.

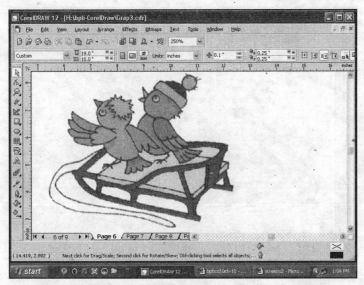

Figure 11.11 A Oil Pastel stroke applied to the image

7. Click the preview button to preview the image.

8. Click OK (See Figure 11.11).

You will observe two small buttons on the top left corner of the Pastel dialog box. These buttons are seen in almost all the effects dialog box. Clicking on the first button will show the before and after applying effect preview of the image. The second image shows the effect in a single preview window. At the top right corner of each of the Effect dialog box, there is a small triangle. Clicking on it will show all the effects available in Bitmaps menu in a drop down menu.

To transform color, do this:

1. Select the image.

2. Click Bitmaps menu, highlight Color Transform and choose from any of the available options (See Figure 11.12).

3. As an example, choose Psychedelic…. The Psychedelic box appears as shown in Figure 11.13.

4. Set the level and Click OK (See Figure 11.14).

To distort images, do this:

1. Select the image.

2. Click Bitmaps menu, highlight Distort and choose from any of the available options (See Figure 11.15).

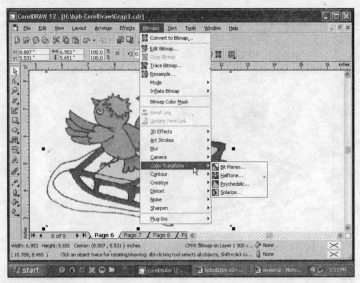

Figure 11.12 The different Color Transform options.

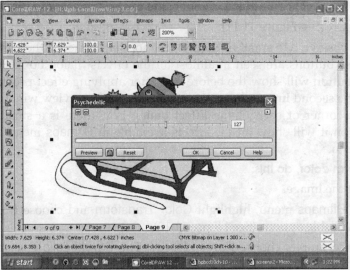

Figure 11.13 The Psychedelic Dialog box

3. As an example, choose Swirl…. The Swirl dialog box appears as shown in Figure 11.16.

4. Select any one of the radio button, Clockwise or Counter-clockwise in which the direction of image twist.

Figure 11.14 A Psychedelic Color Transform Applied to the Image

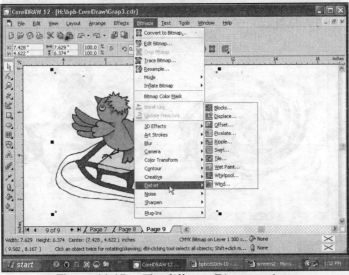

Figure 11.15 The different Distort options

5. In the Angle area, move the slider, at the right corner of the box increase and decrease the size of the **Whole Rotations:** select the fixed angle, to rotates the image.

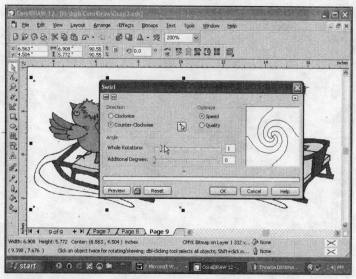

Figure 11.16   Setting Attributes in the Swirl dialog box.

Figure 11.17   Image of the birds (right) has been converted into a twist form.

6. Move the slider, at the right corner of the box to increase or decrease the angle of the **Additional Degrees:** select the fixed degree, to fix the image

7. Click OK (See Figure 11.17)

To add noise, do this:

1. Select the image.
2. Click Bitmaps menu, highlight Noise and choose Add Noise. Add Noise dialog box appears as shown in Figure 11.18.

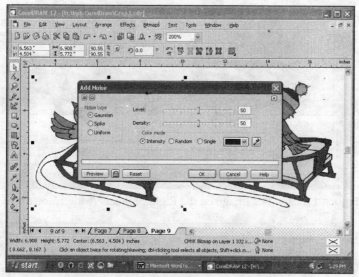

Figure 11.18   The Add Noise Dialog box.

3. Specify noise type in the Noise Type area.
4. Specify level and density by dragging the Level and Density slider respectively.
5. Click OK.
6. Choose a color mode from the Color mode area (See Figure 11.19).

It is not possible to discuss here each and every effect, available for Bitmap images. Experiment with the remaining effects yourself.

Color Masking

Color masking removes pixels having a selected color.

To apply color mask to a bitmap image, do this:

1. Select the image.
2. Click Bitmaps menu and choose Bitmap Color Mask. The Bitmap Color Mask docker appears as in Figure 11.20.

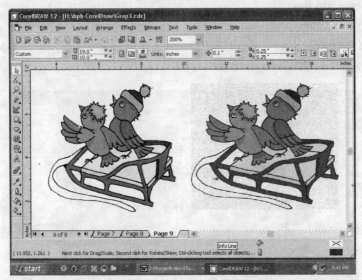

Figure 11.19 The Image on the Right Side has Added Noise to it

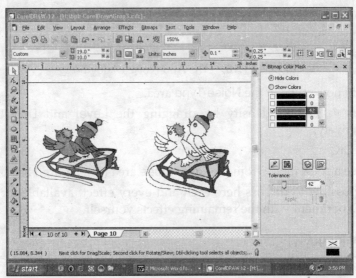

Figure 11.20 The Color Mask docker window. Observe that the inside color of the bird has been removed from the figure

3. Click on the Hide Color option on the docker window.

4. Slide the Tolerance slider to specify the exactness of the color to be removed.

5. Now click the Eyedropper icon and click on the color in the image which is to be removed.

6. You will observe that the chosen color appears in the first bar of the Bitmap Color Mask rollup.

7. When the color in the rollup matches the color you want to delete, then click Apply. Watch that color, and any other similar colored pixels (depending on the Tolerance) disappear.

8. If you need to delete additional colors from your bitmap image, use the remaining bars in the Bitmap Color Mask rollup. But before you click Apply, disable the check boxes next to the color which you do not want to remove.

9. To reset the previous color of the image, click on the Remove Mask button.

Resizing And Rotating /Skewing Images

Images are treated as any other object when it comes to performing transformations on them like resizing, rotating, skewing etc. You are already familiar with transforming objects using the Transformations docker Window. The same process applies for all images, be it Vector or Bitmap image.

Exporting Images

You can export CorelDRAW 12 image to a different file format. This is useful when you want an image to be visible to anyone, even if he does not have a CorelDRAW 12 compatible package. For example, if you want to use an image on a Web Site, you will need to export the image into a GIF or JPG format. In CorelDRAW 12 you can also export an image in PDF format. PDF format is widely accepted for printing and Web based applications.

In addition CorelDraw 12 includes a new features to Export a drawing to the SVG file format. Scalable Vector Graphics (SVG) is an open standard graphics file format that allows designers to put the power of vector graphics to work on the Web. Scalable Vector Graphics are described in Extensible Markup Language (XML). Graphics files have an **.svg** filename extension.

To export to an SVG file, do this:

1. Click File menu and choose Export....

2. In the Export dialog box, select the folder in which you want to save the image in the Save in: drop down menu.

3. Choose the file format in which you want to export the image, in the Saves as type: drop down menu.

4. Click the Scalable vector graphics to save the file.

5. Type a name for your file in the File name: text field and click Export.

6. SVG Export dialog appears as in Figure 11.21.

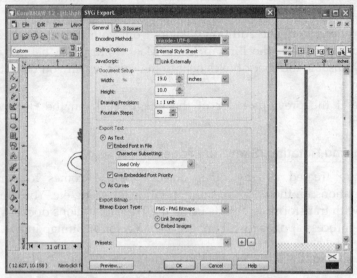

Figure 11.21 SVG Export dialog box

7. From the Encoding Method list choose any one of the following list.

- Unicode-UTF-8 — It is a smaller file size. This is the default encoding method.

- Unicode-UTF-16 — It is a bigger file size.

8. Choose one of the following options from the Styling options list box:

- Internal style sheet — lets you embed the style sheet in the Scalable Vector Graphics file by using the Class attribute.

- Presentation attributes — lets you specify attributes directly in an element in the exported file.

- External CSS — creates an external cascading style sheet file and links it to the Scalable Vector Graphics file.

- If you Select Link externally check box in the JavaScript area. Java script related to overturn and can be saved to a separate file.

9. In the **Document area**, enter a value in the **width:** spin box, and **Height:** spin box.

10. In the **Drawing precision:** list box, select the drawing precision defined as a ratio of units.

11. In the Fountain Steps: box, type the number of fill steps to export. (i.e the shades of color that makes up the appearance of a fountain fill.)

12. In the **Export text** area, enable one of the following options:

    • As text — lets you export text as editable characters, known as single character in a font. You can also Enable the **Embed font in file** check box. Choose which fonts you want to embed from the Character subsetting list box.

    • As curves — lets you export text as curves. You can also Enable the Give embedded font priority check box.

13. In the **Bitmap export type:** list box, choose JPEG, GIF, or PNG file format to export and enable one of the following options.

    • Link images saves each bitmap as a separate file that is linked to the SVG file.

    • Embed images embeds each bitmap in the SVG file.

14. Choose a preset from the **Presets:** list box.

15. Click preview to preview the exported file. To preview the SVG file, you can use the Corel SVG viewer installed with the application. Otherwise the file shows in the Internet Explorer.

CHAPTER 12

Page Layout

Introduction

CorelDRAW 12 allows you to specify the size, orientation, unit of scale and background of the page of drawing. You can customize and display page grids and guidelines to help you to organize objects and place them exactly where you want. For example, if you are designing a newsletter, you can set the dimensions of the pages and create guidelines for positioning columns and heading text. When you are laying out an advertisement, you can align graphics and advertisement copy along guidelines and arrange graphic elements within a grid. Rulers can help you position grids, guidelines, and objects along a scale using units of your choosing. Also, you can add and delete pages of the document.

Layout Styles ·

CorelDRAW lets you choose a preset layout style for a drawing. You can choose the layout style depending on the nature of project you are working on. For example, to design a book, click on the Book style. Other options available in CorelDRAW are Booklet, Tent Card, Side-fold card and Top-fold card. In a multi page document, you can set whether you want the page to appear face to face or not.

To set layout styles for the drawing window, do this:

1. Click the Layout menu and choose Page Setup... . The Options dialog box appears as in Figure 12.1.
2. Click on Layout in the left side of the Options dialog box.
3. In the Layout drop down menu, choose a Layout style.
4. Check the Facing pages check box, if you want the left and right pages to face each other.
5. Click the Start on: list box and choose Left side to start the document on a left facing page. Click the Right side to start the document on a right facing page. The Start on: list box is highlighted only if the Layout chosen is Full page or Book style.

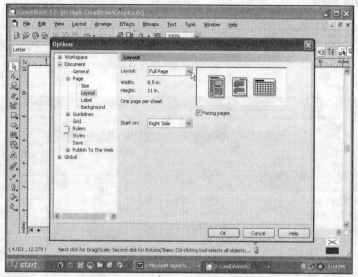

Figure 12.1 Layout tab in the Options dialog box

Define Page Size

The easiest way to define the page size is to click on a blank part of the Drawing area. When you do this, the Page Layout Property Bar becomes active. This Property Bar is also referred to as the No Selection Property Bar as it is active when you do not select any object. You can use this Property Bar to define the size and orientation of the page, as well as many other attributes. (See Figure 12.2)

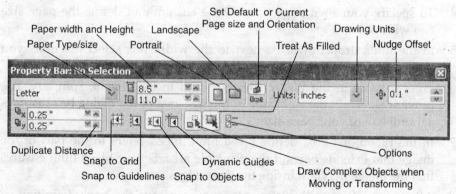

Figure 12.2 No Selection Property Bar

Setting the Size

To set the page size do this:

1. Click Layout menu and choose Page Setup... .
2. Click on Size in the left side of the Options dialog box which appears as in Figure 12.3.

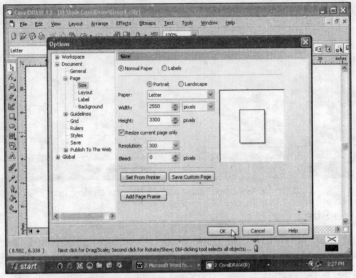

Figure 12.3 Size tab in the Options dialog box

3. When the Size section of the Options dialog box becomes active, click the Paper: list and choose from the standard Page size available.
4. To specify your own page size, choose custom and define the page size and width.
5. In the units drop down list next to the width box select the units you prefer to work with.
6. Enter a value in the Width: spin box, and in the Height: spin box. The preview screen in the right side of the size area of the dialog box displays a thumbnail of your page size.
7. In the Bleed: list box, define bleed limit. Bleed refers to the part of the image that extends beyond the printable area. Setting bleed limit ensures that the image fits right inside the page edges.
8. After you define your custom size, you can save the page definition so that you can use it again. To save your custom page setting, Click on the

Save Custom Page button. The dialog box appears as in Figure 12.4. Provide a name for your page definition.

9. *Alternatively*, click on the **Paper Type/Size** drop-down list in the property bar and choose a paper type and size.

10. Click **OK**.

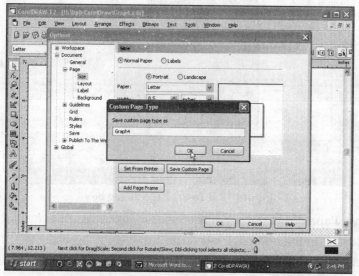

Figure 12.4 Custom Page Type dialog box

Inserting Pages

You can have more than one page in a publication. These pages can either define properties such as page size for a selected page or for all pages.

To insert pages in a publication, do this:

1. Click on the Layout menu, and choose Insert Page. The Insert Page... dialog box appears as in Figure 12.5.

2. Specify how many pages you want to insert in the Insert pages list box.

3. Click the **Before** or **After** radio button to specify where you want the new page(s) to appear.

4. Click the **Portrait** radio button to transform page layout to portrait type that is pages that are taller than they are wide.

5. Click the **Landscape** radio button. To transform the page layout to landscape type that has pages that are wider than they are tall.

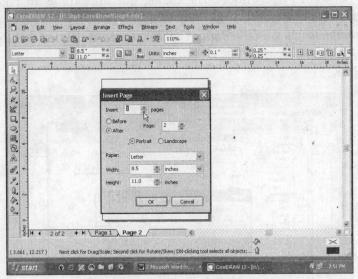

Figure 12.5 Insert Page dialog box

6. Choose Paper: from the paper list box.

7. Select size for the new page in Width: and Height: list box.

8. Select any unit of measurement for your page from Drawing Units list and then click **OK**.

9. You can also switch between the Landscape and Portrait orientation of the layout by clicking on the <u>L</u>ayout menu and choosing Switch Page Orientation.

After you insert pages, you can move from page to page by clicking the page tabs at the bottom of the CorelDRAW window.

The pages inserted can be renamed according to your requirement for easy reference and can also be deleted.

To delete a page, do this:

1. Click the <u>L</u>ayout menu and choose <u>D</u>elete Page.... The Delete Page dialog box appears as in Figure 12.6.

2. In the Delete page: list box, type the page number of the page you want to delete.

3. To delete multiple pages, click the Through to page: check box, and set the page number up to which you want to delete, in the list box.

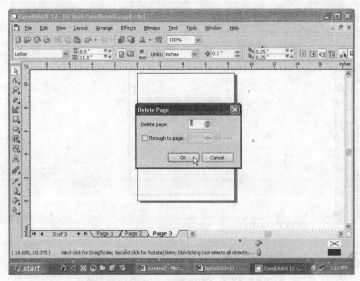

Figure 12.6 Delete Page dialog box

To rename a page, do this:

1. Move to the page which you want to rename.

2. Click the Layout menu and choose Rename Page.... The Rename Page dialog box appears as in Figure 12.7.

3. In the Page name: box, type the new name for the page. The current page will be renamed with this new name.

Specifying Background Color

You can specify the background color of a page. You can apply a solid color for background if you want a uniform background to the page or you can even apply a bitmap image as a background for your page.

To apply background color, do this:

1. Click Layout menu and choose Page Background... .

2. Click the Background in the left side of the Options dialog box as in Figure 12.8.

3. Click the Solid radio button.

4. Click the Color picker and choose a color from the drop down list.

5. Click OK.

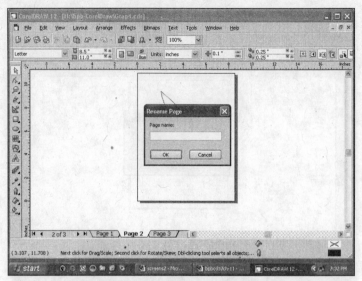

Figure 12.7 Rename Page dialog box

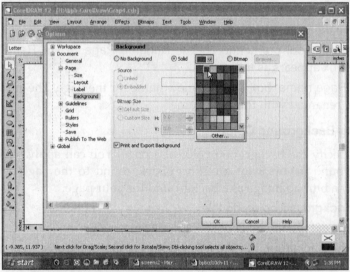

Figure 12.8 Background tab in the Options dialog box

To apply a bitmap image as background, do this:

1. In the Background dialog box (See Figure 12.8), click the Bitmap radio button.

2. The Options in the dialog box are shown in Figure 12.9.

3. Click **Browse...** button.

4. Choose a file format from the **Files of type:** list box. Locate the file where the bitmap image you want as Background, is stored.

5. If you choose **Linked** option, the changes you do in the source file will be reflected in the bitmap image background.

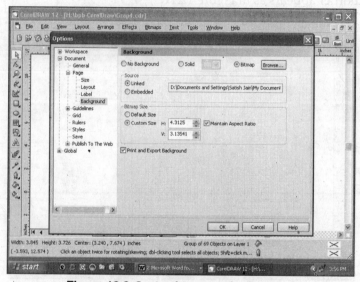

Figure 12.9 Setting bitmap as background

6. If you choose **Embedded**, the changes made in the source file will not be reflected.

7. If you want the background to be printable and exportable, enable the **Print and Export Background** check box.

8. Click on the **Default Size**, to let CorelDRAW 12 tile or crop the image to fit the page.

9. Click on **Custom Size** to specify the dimensions of the bitmapped image. Type values in the H: and V: boxes.

To remove a background, do this:

1. Click the **Layout** menu and choose **Page Background....**

2. Click the **No Background** radio button.

Hiding the page border

To hide the page border, do this:

1. Click the T<u>o</u>ols menu and choose <u>O</u>ptions.... The Options dialog box appears as in Figure 12.10.
2. Click Page on the left side of the Options dialog box.
3. On the right side, check the Show page border. Check box to show the page border appears as in Figure 12.11.

Figure 12.10   Page tab in the Options dialog box

4. Check the Show printable area to indicate the printable area. (See Figure 12.11.
5. Check the Show bleed area to display the bleed and printable area on the drawing window. (See Figure 12.11)

Going to specific pages

To go to a specific page, do this:

1. Click the <u>L</u>ayout menu and choose <u>G</u>o To Page... . The Go To Page dialog appears as in Figure 12.12.
2. In the Go to Page dialog box, choose the specified page from the Go To Page; list box and click OK.
3. *Alternatively*, you can move to a specific page, by pressing at the page tab located in the bottom left of the CorelDRAW window.

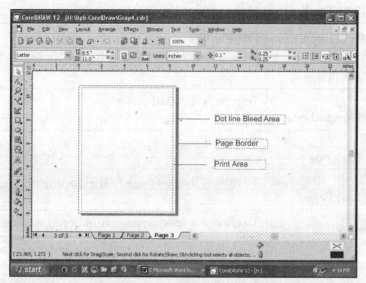

Figure 12.11   This Figure showing bleed area, page border and print area

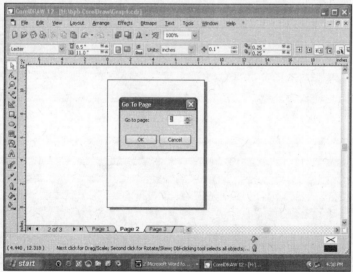

Figure 12.12   Go To Page dialog box

4. The facilities provided by the page tab are also known as Document Navigator and are given in Table 12.1.

Table 12.1 The Buttons in Document Navigator

Name	Description
◄ First Page	To moves the first page in the document.
► Forward one	To moves forward one page.
◄ Back one	To moves back page.
►I Last Page	To moves the last page in the document.
Page 2	To choose a specific page number to go page 2
+	Click left + (plus) button to add page at the beginning, and right + (plus) button to add page at the end.

CHAPTER 13

Printing and Publishing Options

Introduction

CorelDRAW 12 comes with a full set of printer options to make it easy for printing business cards, labels, and other odd-sized output. In CorelDRAW 12, you can print one or more copies of the same drawing. You can specify what to print, as well as which parts of a drawing to print. For example, you can print selected vectors, bitmaps, text, or layers. Before printing a drawing, you can specify printer properties, including paper size and device options.

Selecting a Printer

To select a printer do this:

1. Click the <u>F</u>ile menu and choose <u>P</u>rint... . The Print dialog box appears as in Figure 13.1.

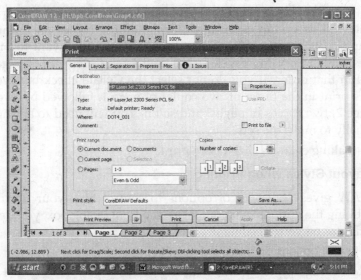

Figure 13.1 Print dialog box

2. Click the General Tab.
3. Select a printer in the Name: list box.
4. In the Print Range area, the options are:

Current document – To print all the pages in your document, click the current document radio button.

Current Page – To print the active page in your document, click the Current page radio button.

Pages – To print range of pages, say, pages 1 to 20 in a 50 page document, type the first page number and then select the desired page number in the **Pages:** radio button. Separate the numbers with hyphens like 1-20.

In the **Pages** drop down list, select the desired pages you want.

Documents – To print more than one document at a time click this radio button.

Selection – To print the selected text, first select it, and then click the **Selection** radio button. This option is dimmed unless you have selected something in your document.

5. In the Copies area, the options are:

Number of copies: – Specify the number of copies of the document you want to print in the number of copies list box.

Collate – This option determines how multiple copies are printed. For example, if you have a four-page document and you want to print two copies, collating prints pages 1, 2, 3, and 4, and then prints pages 1,2,3, and 4 in that order. If you do not select the **Collate** check box, your two copies print in the order of two copies of page 1, followed by two copies of page 2, two copies of page 3 and so on. You will need to arrange them manually to make the sets.

6. After making changes click OK to print.

Using Layout Styles when Printing

CorelDRAW gives you a lot of options to control how your document is printed. Using the options in layout tab of the **Print** dialog box, you define the print attributes on your document.

To select layout options do this:

1. Create a Paragraph text frame with any object.

2. Click the <u>F</u>ile menu and choose <u>P</u>rint.... The Print dialog box appears.

3. Click the Layout tab property sheet appears as in Figure 13.2.

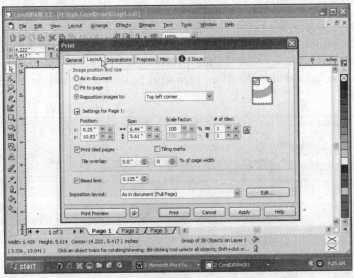

Figure 13.2 Layout tab in the Print dialog box

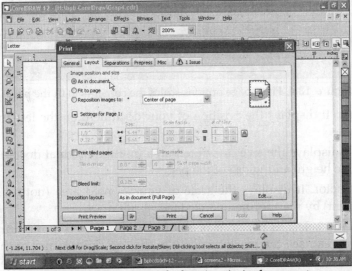

Figure 13.3 Layout tab showing As in document

4. There are three ways to treat the position and size of layout.

5. As in document – Click this radio button, to print your document as it is without any modification. (See Figure 13.3)

6. **Fit to page** – Click this radio button, to scale the image so that it fits the printable page. (See Figure 13.4).

7. **Reposition images to** – Click this radio button to place the printed image as per your requirement. In the position, specified in the list box on the right side, adjust the Position, Size and Scale values below it. (See Figure 13.5)

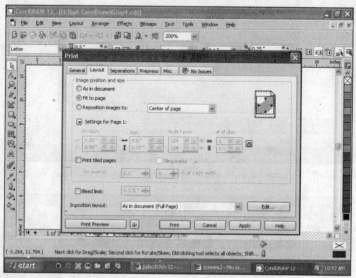

Figure 13.4 Fit to page options scales the contents to fit the page

Position: It displays the position of your document on the left and top of the page.

Size: It displays the size of printed area (not the original document) and gives the height and width of the page.

Scale factor: It displays the scale of your printed area (not the original document) by the specified percentage.

8. When you select as per your need of options selected in the print dialog box, you can see the small preview at the top right corner of the dialog box. Or at the bottom of the print preview button, you can see a small double rectangle button. Click this button and you can see the preview.

Tiling a Print Job

Tiling feature is useful when you want to print a drawing which is larger than the paper your printer can print. So using this feature, CorelDRAW tiles

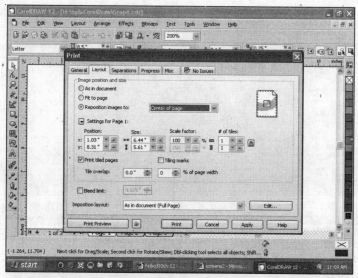

Figure 13.5 Reposition images to option lets you position drawing on the print page

your document. You can then print these tiles and assemble them to get the document.

To tile a print job do this:

1. Click the File menu and choose Print... .

2. Click the Layout tab.

3. Click the Print tiled pages check box. This enables you to print large print jobs on multiple sheets, or tiles, that can be assembled later to form the entire document. Type values in the list boxes.

   Tile overlap: – specify the number of inches by which to overlap tiles.

   % of page width: – specify the percentage of the page width, the tiles will occupy.

   # of tiles: – let you specify the number of horizontal and vertical tiles on the page.

4. Click the Tiling marks check box. This enable to include tiling alignment marks.

5. Click the Print Preview button as show in Figure 13.6.

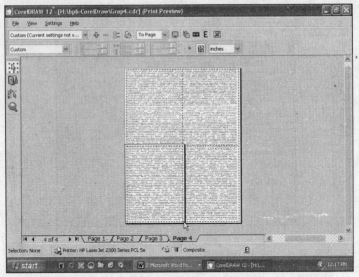

Figure 13.6 Print tiled pages showing Print Preview

Using Print Style

A print style is a set of saved printing options. Each print style is a separate file. This lets you move a print style from one machine to another, back up a print style, and keep document specific styles in the same folder as the document file.

You can select a print style or edit a print style and save such changes. You can also delete print styles.

To edit a print style do this:

1. Click the File menu and choose Print... .
2. Choose a Print style, from the Print style: list box. The Print dialog box appears as in Figure 13.7.
3. Choose any of the Ready made style.

To save print style do this:

1. In the Print dialog box, click the Save As... button.
2. The Save Settings As dialog box appears as in Figure 13.8.
3. In Save in: list box choose the drive and folder where the print style is stored. (See Figure 13.8)

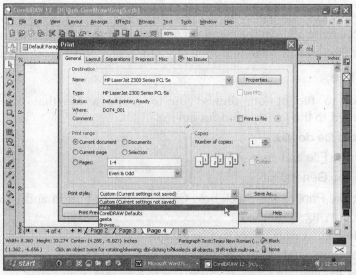

Figure 13.7 Print dialog box showing the Print Style list

Figure 13.8 Save Setting As dialog box

4. Click the filename in the **File name:** list box.
5. Click **Save** button.

To delete a print style do this:

1. Click the File menu and chose Print Preview... .
2. Select a print style in the standard toolbar.
3. Click the Delet print style button (i.e. Minus sign (--)).

Print to File

The Print to file option allows you to create a file that can later be downloaded to the selected output device.

To print to a file do this:

1. Click the File and choose Print... .
2. Click the General tab.
3. Click the Print to file check box. Click the flyout button and choose from the following options.

   Single File – prints pages to a single file

   Pages to separate files – prints pages to separate files.

   Plates to separate files – prints plates to separate files.

4. Click OK.